Jonathan Sturges

History of the Class of' '85, of Princeton College.

Jonathan Sturges

History of the Class of' '85, of Princeton College.

ISBN/EAN: 9783337170578

Printed in Europe, USA, Canada, Australia, Japan

Cover: Foto ©ninafisch / pixelio.de

More available books at **www.hansebooks.com**

THE CLASS OF '85,

—OF—

PRINCETON COLLEGE.

By JONATHAN STURGES, Class Historian.

——JUNE, 1885.——

TRENTON, N. J.:
MacCrellish & Quigley, Book and Job Printers, 10 East State Street.

1885.

To · my · Classmates · I · dedicate

this · Book,

Written · for · their · pleasure · and · my · own.

J. S.

PRINCETON, June 15, 1885.

CLASS HISTORY.

CLARENCE J. ALLEN, Philadelphia, Pa.

Usually known as "Calf," and thereby hangs a tale. In order to check the abominable presumption and tone down the overweening spirit manifested by the worthless Class of '84, a few choice spirits, Arthur Tree and Harry Thorp among them, had decided to hire a small white jackass which they had seen grazing in the fields of a farmer near Princeton, paint a green '84 upon his side and tie him to the cannon that all College, as they came out of morning Chapel, might see him—a fitting type of '84. Unfortunately the Sophomores got wind of this, and proceeded to get off what we in our Freshmen days were wont to call a honeyman. *Mutatis mutanda*, however, of course, the figures '85 were substituted and imprinted upon the body of an innocent calf, which was tied to the Chapel door. That morning "Calf" Allen, *horribile dictu*, cut Chapel the first time, the first step in a long career of vice; but it proved the saving of the Class. As he came up from breakfast he saw the calf, and, fired with patriotic zeal, he rushed up. After a fierce struggle with that stalwart giant, Ben Butler, who was standing guard, he untied the bovine and drove it away in time, but was known as "Calf" ever after. "Calf" was a boy of uncertain tendencies; in fact, one might say of him that he never knew exactly what he was going to do next, or how long he would stick at it. He remained with us but a year, and then joined '86 Scientif; but he soon tired of so narrow a field, and at present writing is reported as doing well in the Altoona workshops, raising a full beard and becoming learned in the manners and customs of the Pennsylvania Dutch.

GEORGE B. ANDERSON, Washington, D. C.

We all thought George was a *blasé*, worn-out man of the world, as we saw him appear on the Campus, one of the few among us who sported whiskers and a mustache. He had been at West Point; he had been at the University of Virginia; he had been a student in Germany—the dear knows where he hadn't been. To be sure, his career at any of these places had not been particularly brilliant or lengthy, but he had seen life; that was all that was necessary. How we used to listen, with eager pride, to reports of his lying in bed at Mrs. Smith's, driving nails (so the story ran) into the door at ten yards' distance with his revolver, which had stood him in so many fights. The poor landlady complained to the Faculty, and George's little freak was visited with several disorder marks. What a martyr! Then, too, who can forget the way George ran in his ticket at the Freshman class-meeting. Most of us didn't know what a ticket was, but " it was strange the way all that crowd got elected, wasn't it?" However, we soon got to know George, and so did the Faculty. His stay here was not long. He " left " at Christmas, and the place thereof shall know him no more.

RICHARD H. APPLEBY, New York City.

Often called " Our Harry;" not " Old Harry," for Appleby in no wise resembled that gentleman, being of a gay and innocent turn of mind. Appleby was one of those men who gained prominence chiefly by the seat in class which was assigned him on the alphabetical system. Just think, after Allen and Anderson left he could say, " I am first in my class," and so he was, for he sat first. And when Chet. came! Oh, great unparalleled honor, to sit next the American Prince of Wales! It was noticed that Appleby procured himself a nice new check suit at Leigh's and wore it daily to class till the novelty of the presence of his distinguished neighbor wore off.

CHESTER ALLAN ARTHUR, New York City.

" Chet.," " The Prince," " The Heir Apparent," etc., etc. When " Chet." first came among us, a rather ludicrous scene was enacted. It was first term, Sophomore year. The President had arrived, heralded by the newspapers a week in advance. We all assembled on the lawn in front of the President's house, from the steps of which the President was to make a speech. After a few remarks, he said: "I feel affection for Princeton. How great my trust you may judge from the fact that I am about to leave the *most precious thing I have on earth* in your care." We all stood silent. Jimmy got very nervous. At last we understood what was wanted, and set up a tremendous cheer, inwardly resolving to *take care* of that most precious thing if it attempted any "funny business" in the way of being better than the rest of us. We didn't care if he was the President's son; rather the reverse, in fact. Arthur came among us under a disadvantage—we were prejudiced against him; a visible effect of our glorious democratic institutions. But Arthur, though he never knew many of us very well, turned out a pleasant enough, quiet fellow, and in the end received from the Class the honor of a place on the Class-Day Committee. Poor Arthur's years in College used to be enlivened about every other day by some delightful little newspaper squib about Young Arthur this, Young Arthur that; Young Arthur is about to be shipped; Young Arthur is about to stand head of his Class; Young Arthur is about to marry Miss So-and-so; Young Arthur has broken Miss What-do-you-call-em's heart, etc., etc. These used to afford a good deal of amusement to the rest of the Class, and were a source of secret pride to "Chet." himself, who was reported to cut them all out and paste them in his scrap-book. So nice to be first in the "upper-ten" of America, you know. Among his intimates, his Cabinet as it were, "Chet." was fond of telling of how he once visited the Governor-General and the Princess Louise in Canada. "I used to sit next the Princess at dinner," he used to say, "and the Princess used to talk a good deal to me, and I used to go boating with the Princess, and when the Princess went out sketching I used to carry the Princess's easel. Dreadful bore, you know, but friendly relations between the two countries must be kept up, and— By the way, the Princess has a horse she would like to sell, and I can get it for you as a great favor, I think—only $1,500—the Princess being a personal friend of mine. By the way, as the Princess used—" But here his friends would usually contrive to introduce some taking subject, such as some good old bourbon, and the conversation would cease for the time.

JOHN M. AUSTIN, Philadelphia, Pa.

Known as "Tone," and chiefly for being "tone," his chief business in life appearing to be to wear his clothes right, and have a good time generally. The course proved too difficult for "Tone." He left us at the end of first term, Junior year, and has never come back.

ALRED T. BAKER, B.S., Camden, N. J.

"Alfy" did a good deal for our Class. He was one of our best Freshmen foot-ball players, got on the 'Varsity in his Sophomore year, to our joy and pride, and remained a crack player on the team till he was graduated. He played in the Harvard game, but was unable to play in the Yale game on account of a sprained ankle. The same thing happened in our Senior year, when he was making his great tear. "Alfy" was on the Glee Club, also, for three years, and had much to do with making the strength and reputation of '85.

WILLIAM SEBASTIAN GRAFF BAKER, B.S., Baltimore, Md.

William Sebastian's legs were very long, like his name, and it was these unfortunately long legs which got him into trouble. He was easily recognized by them; in fact, he was the only man in the Class who possessed lower appendages of such length and thinness. Every one remembers William Sebastian on the foot-ball field. When once in motion, heated with enthusiasm, and shouting to the Freshmen scrub to back him up (he wasn't Captain of the scrub, but he ought to have been), nothing but at least three feathers could cause those long legs to bend and cast their owner to the ground. On that memorable night before Marquand's Latin examination in Freshman year, the night of the horn-spree, William Sebastian sallied forth among the rest, well disguised, as he thought, by a mask; but of all that jovial company he was the only one recognized by the watchman, who said he knew him by his stature or legs, which could not be masked. The result was that poor William Sebastian was hauled up before Mayor Hageman, and gave away not only himself but the names of his associates, who were all rusticated. The Class was very angry at the time, and would have made it exceedingly unpleasant for William Sebastian had he ever returned to College. Purchasing one's own safety at the expense of one's classmates is a thing not to be approved of, but it must be remembered that Mayor Hageman used sharp practice with poor Baker; he actually went so far as to threaten him with State's Prison unless he disclosed the names, and effectually scared the prisoner out of his wits. Mayor Hageman's whole course through this affair was resented by the College as unworthy of the Mayor of Princeton and actuated by a spirit of animosity and unfairness towards the College. The students showed their feeling at the next election, when Mr. Hageman was defeated, the College votes being cast against him.

JOHN W. BARR, Louisville, Ky.

John was as popular a man as there was in the Class. In spite of the general slaughter of Ivy candidates at the Class elections, he was the first elected to the Class-Day Committee; went in with a "whoop," as they say, to the satisfaction of all. Perhaps the reason of his popularity was that, unlike most of the Western expedition fiends, he brought back no store of Indian talk to burden his friends with, only some rattles and a few good stories on Scott, which he was wont to tell with great unction.

CHARLES H. BATEMAN, Pennington, N. J.

Like a shade he vanished, and the historian never knew him.

JAMES WILSON BAYARD, Philadelphia, Pa.

"Wilsy" he was called at home, but this name was soon lost for that of "Fuzzy," presumably given with reference to that beard of light color and extremely thin texture which was his joy and pride, and which contrasted well with his otherwise youthful appearance. Razor had never touched his cheeks, he boasted, and many were the plans concocted and the oaths sworn that it should ere Freshman year were over. Josy Bangs and George Young, being slightly under the influence one night, purchased false noses and mustaches at Priest's, secured a dull razor and visited "Fuzzy's" room in the University at dead of night, or rather when the night was nearly dead, for knowing their victim's early habits (he always went to bed at nine and rose at six), they hoped to find him sleeping. But, alas! "Fuzzy" had broken his rule; it was ten o'clock and he had not finished his devotions, and when he saw those strange, weird, unknown forms enter his chamber, smoking pipes, the odor of which was his abhorrence, he rose in his wrath and in his night-gown, and stood with wild eyes and asked their names and for what fell and murderous purpose they had invaded the 'sanctity of his apartment, and bade them leave it. But they would not. So "Fuzzy" laid hands upon Josy and endeavored to eject him forcibly, trying as it was to his modesty to parade in such abbreviated costume. So they struggled till at last they both fell to earth, and great was the mirth of Josy's accomplice as he saw him very angry, very red in the face, rolling upon the floor, spitting and swearing, while the virtuous "Fuzzy" thundered out the anathemas of scripture. And when Josy was about to prevail, for he was strong, lo! the false nose and mustachios came off and "Fuzzy" knew him and threatened him with the Faculty and he fled.

Also, when he came to College was it "Fuzzy's" ambition to stand at the head of the Class, and he had formed a theory that men of mighty intellects had large heads, and that the man with the largest head would have the mightest intellect, and would, therefore, be sure and stand first; therefore, before risking any shekels in betting on himself for first honor man, did "Fuzzy" measure his own head and compare it with those of Knapp, Edwards, etc., his cronies, and found that he was *facile princeps*. Then did "Fuzzy" try conclusions with C. & W. McIlvaine, those mighty men, and again was he *makro cephalous*. So great was the joy and expectation in "Fuzzy's" heart, but he was doomed to disappointment, and, at the Christmas examination, his stand was number two instead of number one. "Fuzzy" has abandoned his theory now, and says he doesn't think there is very much in phrenology after all.

ROBERT H. BEATTIE, New Hurley, N. Y.

Beattie was always a good youth, faithful in his "polling," regular in his attendance at recitations and the Philadelphian. No grinds are there on Beattie; always did he walk the straight and narrow path, from which he only deviated on occasional mashing forays, which left no trace on Beattie's hardened heart. How it did fill his mind with joy and pride to conduct a bevy of fair maidens over the Campus, and show them all the sights, from the gymnasium—where, of a hot summer's day, there would be but a single athlete, probably the immortal Sampson Brann, balancing on the bar as usual—to the Old Chapel, gray with the dust of ages. With what reverence and awe was he looked up to as, with an air of pompous mystery, he pointed out the sacred shades of Clio Hall. "That's the place where they play tennis when we're not studying; and that little building among the evergreens there? oh, that's a sort of a tool-house, you know." Never mind, Beattie; have we not all done the same? From one you may learn all. But stop! Did I say that he never strayed away? Ah, yes, once; once, alas! and, though he repented in ashes and returned, never will he be the same innocent youth again. Knapp was the "child of sin who took him by the forelock and led him in," and under Knapp's name and to his account be the shame told.

JOSEPH D. BEDLE, Jr., Jersey City, N. J.

Why wast thou called "Nelly?" Was it because of thy peach-like bloom and that innocent air, in such contrast to that of the hardened "Benny," thy brother? or was it because of some peculiarly feminine characteristic, of which only thy intimates knew? Jo was not prominent in the Class till about the end of second term, Fresh year, when it began to be rumored about that he had had an article printed in the *Princetonian*. Jo did not deny the implication, but blushed with becoming modesty when therewith charged. What an honor! That one of our Class should see his words, the product of his muse, in print! Praise and envy there could not be enough for Jo. Yet some unfeeling wag, in the week when the new editors were to be announced, sent Jo a notice that he was among the elect.

Great was the rejoicing then in Jo's unsuspecting heart. In a fit of generosity he ordered a supper, an excellent, in fact a magnificent supper, in honor of the event, and to this supper he invited his cronies, his tormentor among the number. Loud was the singing, unstinted was the meat and drink, and next morning the hoax was exposed, and sorrow filled Jo's heart at thought of many shekels gone to thunder in vain. But the letter proved true in prophecy, if not in fact. Jo tried for the *Princetonian*, and he got on. Fired with ambition at this success, there was never a contest thereafter of any kind, sort, shape or description in which Jo did not try and—get left. The fellows used to pity Jo a good deal on this account partly, partly because he had to run the Here and There column in the *Princetonian*, Senior year, and partly because of his ill health. It was so hard on him, you know, to be obliged to go away just before examinations, when he would, undoubtedly, have secured a high grade. So unpleasant for him to go South for a couple of months every second term when he could have had such a gay time here. How some of his friends did wish they could spare him such pain, and take his troubles on their shoulders! Poor Jo's brain became so weak on account of his protracted ill health that he actually went so far as to plead, as an excuse to the Faculty for not passing a Psychology examination, "I have but one lung left, gentlemen, upon my honor!" an excuse which, it is needless to state, was found insufficient.

WILLIAM D. BELL, at Large.

Yes, Billy was a "crank," there's no doubt about that; but he's a mighty nice fellow all the same. A crank about what? Why, on the subject of foot-ball. But, if Billy hadn't been a crank on this subject, '85 would never have had a team capable of taking the championship from Yale. Billy was captain of the scrub in Senior year. He didn't play much of a game himself, and his runs, when he saw Kid Toler or Birdie making for him with extended arms, were apt to be in the direction of his own goal. On this account he was the subject of much teasing, but the work he did in bringing out a good scrub, at much pains to himself, without missing a single day, was recognized by the Class. They gave him a place on the Class-Day Committee, and forgave all his short-comings. Do you remember the language you used when you received one of Brackett's notelets in Junior year, Billy? I had intended to expose you, but refrain.

THOMAS C. BERRY, Baltimore, Md.

Tom was a quiet boy, who was in the habit of polling himself into a brain fever once in a while by way of diversion. The historian chiefly remembers him for having produced the first impression ever made on Thorpey's maiden heart. It was commonly reported at the time that they were engaged. Tom left us at the end of Sophomore year, and is now in California, sheep ranching, as I hear.

EDMUND W. BILL, B.S., New York City.

Bill was one of that sort of men denominated a "queer fellow." Every one insisted, therefore, that there must be lots of grinds on him. No trouble about that, every one said, and his friends would laugh with a superior air of amusement whenever application was made to them. Bill may have possessed a fierceness in his private relations which cowed his cronies and made them fear to disclose his secrets; more likely, however, it is that he had none. In Freshman year, Bill was of a bold and yet a nervous nature. He went out on the Track-Greasing Expedition (not to the West), and was among the foremost in depositing the oily fluid upon the rails. Yet that night he tossed and turned and slept not for nervousness and rattledom of the fate that was to come. Yes, Bill was inclined to rattle. Yet his training in self-possession before an audience, which he got in the Glee Club in Junior year, apparently freed him from this trouble. However, in Senior year was he again attacked. He swore he could not stand before that audience at Commencement and read his thesis. "It would make him blush," he said; so to save his blushes and his modest purity, he devised a scheme—keen of a keenness, infamously sharp. Under the planet Uranus was the scheme concocted. Let him know that I only spare him for this History's sake.

CLINTON WALLACE BIRD, New York City.

Birdie's career here was essentially athletic. He never went much into literature, with the exception of the time when he was engaged in an animated controversy with Richards, of Yale, over the foot-ball championship, and was a valued contributor to the pages of the *Evening Post.* The first time I ever saw Birdie was by moonlight. He was clad in a blue-and-white Jersey, was looking very much scared, and was under the protecting care of Bob Spier, '83. Of course it was the night of the 6th of October, 1881, the night of the preliminary cane-spree. Birdie was matched against Frank Miller, '84, and, strange to say, lost his cane after a stubborn fight. If Birdie had been able to get another chance at Miller when he had got over his Freshman scare, the subsequent proceedings would have interested the gentleman of the auburn locks no more, I imagine. Birdie was on the crew from his Freshman year, if that was much of an honor, and was captain in his Junior year. He got on the foot-ball team in his Sophomore year, and was captain in Senior year, when his best playing was done. Being head of the champion foot-ball team, he was honored with the position of Master of Ceremonies at the Class elections, according to precedent.

GRANT R. BENNETT, Portage, Wis.

Bennett blew among us from some little western College at the beginning of Sophomore year. Blew is the right word. He did *blow;* blew extensively. He bet on the foot-ball team, " went round with the boys," was " free with his dollars," as a *World* reporter would put it, and was commonly called " James Gordon" on that account. Most of us only knew him as one of the toughs till, towards the end of the year, he began to make speeches in Hall, and it was noised about that he was a great Shakespearean reader and critic. He started a literary club, and soon gained a good deal of reputation for ability, leading as it were a double sort of life. He had more reputation, perhaps, than he deserved at first; but it glided away from him. Ability he had at bottom, there is no doubt, but the charlatan speeches and actions he perpetrated cast a cloud over it. Shall we ever forget his rising inflection, his downward point with the fingers of the left hand, while in the other he held a big cigar, and declared that he would stand by some thing or other "till the stars grow cold," etc.? Hundreds of absences and other unpleasant things did he accumulate. He staid to deliver his oration, and departed to return no more. Latest reports from the West say that he has nearly finished a year at law, has a novel under way, and has completed the dramatization of Dickens' "Tale of Two Cities." Success to him in his varied enterprise.

JOHN BENNETT BISSELL, Jr., Charleston, S. C.

Jack's career here was essentially athletic, yet not preëminently so. He tried for everything and was very much offended when the base-ball men requested him to stop practicing, as he took time from the others. Jack thought there was something personal about this, so he abandoned athletics, set up for a "dude," and joined Jim Potter's crowd. He left us at the end of Sophomore year, and went to Harvard for a time, where he acquired considerable reputation as having been a famous pitcher at Princeton. From Harvard he drifted away and further is not known.

EDWARD KING BLADES, Watseka, Ill.

King was noted for being the most positive man on the face of the earth. I mean positive that his own way was right in athletics, in studies, in everything you can think of. As Ben Smith was equally positive, and was exceedingly loud in his conversation, the fellows at Dohm's used to think the house would come down when King and Ben got arguing at the table, and the Freshmen used to come out of their rooms, with their innocent faces, wondering what was the matter. In these discussions logic was not King's forte, as those who remember his famous syllogism in Jeremy Bentham will be ready to believe. The syllogism ran about as follows: "All men are mortal. All trade-winds are hot. ∴ The Hottentots wear no clothes."

SAMUEL McCREA BRANN, Charlton, N. Y.

"Sampson" he was called, from his strength (he was fond of spending hours balancing in the gym.), or from his hair, which was copious. He kept very quiet. There were no grinds on him except one which the fellows at his club endeavored to pound into the historian's head, but the point of which he remains ignorant to this day. He entered Junior year, and he came from Union.

JOHN W. BLYE, Philadelphia, Pa.

Great was the rejoicing and many the blessings showered on Jack's head that memorable night of the preliminary cane spree. He captured a cane for the honor of '85 from Parmly, '84, and we all rushed up and carried him, by the still light of the moon, on our shoulders to his room. Too much could not be said for Jack, yet never did any one suspect him of being likely to stand at the head of his Class. His capabilities in that line were not great, yet there is record of how once he did deceive poor Goose Gibby, as he was called, into thinking Jack a high-stand man. It was at the Freshman examination in June, the last day. Gibby and Jack were walking up the path by the Old Chapel, and Jack confided to Gibby that Granny Hunt had just told him he passed the finest paper in English he had ever had the pleasure of reading. Gibby listened with open and respectful ears, and "Cam.," who happened to be walking behind them, stepped up. He caught Jack by the hand and wrung it forcibly. "Allow me to congratulate you, my dear young friend, on your having commenced your course so well. I see, I am sure I see, the fire of genius in your eye, and let me give you one caution. In this College those who expectorate on my floor need not expect to rate high in their Class." It was fortunate that Jack, who was a Scientif, had happened to meet "Cam." in this way; he might otherwise never have heard this joke, the one ewe lamb which "Cam." perennially, "on glorious morns," visits upon the Freshmen. Not knowing this, Jack was well content, and kept his hand tightly clasped over his heart, where lay the condition which Granny had sent him that morning. Jack left us at the end of Sophomore year.

JOHN W. BROWN, Milton, Pa.

There is no lack of news items about John W. Brown—I beg his pardon, J. Woods Brown. Unluckily for him he belonged to a crowd whose victuals and drink were grinds on each other, all of which they delighted to pour into the historian's ears. If I were to do him up brown, as the saying goes, I should have had to buy note-books and note-books till my pocket was empty. Jim Buckelew and Griff, who didn't like being teased themselves very well, by the way, never let Brown alone, and, it must be confessed, he gave them ample opportunity. We will all be able to picture him to ourselves in after years, with his broad good-humored face and his carpet trousers—two prominent features. Brown had also a broad Dutch accent, which the fellows at the club were never tired of mimicking. He was always known as the Pennsylvania Dutchman, and the fellows were fond of asking him how things were getting along home at the Cross Roads. Whether anybody had driven into town lately on the ox-cart, or when they were going to kill pigs, etc., etc. Slurs on his domestic surroundings, which Brown never took the trouble to deny, answering invariably when anything of the kind was gotten off, "Pung! Fatal stab! See me bleed!" or "Shut the box," two expressions which you could always draw out of Brown by simply pulling the right string. Oh, the breaks that poor boy used to make, and the slips in grammar, none of which were ever allowed to pass unnoticed. As when Brown would insist that he had seen that girl *already yet*, or ask why '84 sang Bingen on the Rhine for their class ode. Machiavelli was a friend of Brown's, and he also showed great discernment in putting one of the machines in Prof. Young's observatory to use in measuring the force of the *wind*. In Latin once he spoke of the *whining* of the horses, and, when corrected by the laughter of the class, stammered out, "I mean *nai*." Many were the stabs on Brown, which none but the initiated would understand, and I forbear the recital. There were two things to which Brown aspired, namely, to stand high without polling and to be what they called at Stonaker's a society idiot. Both of these objects he attained in a moderate degree in Senior year. At any rate he stood high, and always insisted when he appeared, after being buried in the seclusion of his room for an afternoon or evening, that he had been reading a novel. Jim and Griff would meet this assertion with openly avowed skepticism, but this mattered not to Brown's calm mind. What did he care; did he not get 99.8 in Jimmy McCosh, and work a keen scheme on Charley Shields? One afternoon when all the society idiots were skating on the pond Brown was observed on the scene of action, sauntering up and down, dressed in his new spring overcoat, kid gloves, and those well-known carpet pants. No effect. No hearts were softened. No eyes were turned in his direction. Brown grew cynical after this, and, when the Nassau rink was opened, was wont to frequent that place of vice and skate with ladies of the demi *mode*, as Jim Buckelew called them. This daring course drew eyes upon him, he must be reformed. One evening Bob Sterry went into Brown's room [that was before he roomed in Witherspoon, and carried oil and coal for his Freshman, you know], and found Brown arraying himself in his Sunday best, clean collar, and everything that was extravagant. At last he had received an invitation. Turning to Bowery with a broad and delighted grin, he ejaculated the following sentence: "I'm goin' among 'em." It was not generally known that Brown loved poetry, but such was the case. His favorite poem was the "Ivy Green." Lines from this he would quote at all hours, such as, " Of right choice food are his meals, I ween, in his cell so grand and bold," or " The stateliest building man can raise is the Ivy's home at last." He used to say that he coincided with these sentiments and held them to be strictly true. Alas! the Ivy ingratitude never twined around Brown, perhaps because the tower of his strength was not yet old enough. Yet Brown still loved the dainty plant nevertheless; so much so that he came to identify himself with it, and when nine leaves from the old stock were contesting on the base-ball field with nine lambs from Mamma's fold, Brown was there, watching with eager eyes; and, when the nine leaves scored a winning run, Brown leaped for joy, and called out in triumphant accents, " We're beating! we're beating!"

HENRY C. BRYAN, Washington, D. C.

In Junior year, he entered our Class from Dartmouth. He polled little, he "mashed" much, and he played second base on the Stonaker nine.

JAMES BUCKELEW, C.E., Jamesburg, N. J.

If ever a College man was king anywhere, Jim certainly was at Stonaker's, with Griff. as his prime minister. All the club bowed down to him, and he ruled them with a rod of iron. None must speak while Jim had the floor, and conversation must cease when Jim chose to take a hand and deliver his opinions on some weighty point. The fellows at the other end of the table were fond of having little discussions among themselves, but they were always careful to speak under their breath, for if Jim happened to hear any statement offered with which he did not coincide, he would cut in with crushing force, even the Sophomores at the other table not being safe. Jim was fond of inculcating daily certain rules of moral and social behavior, which he never took the trouble to apply in his own case. If any one spoke while he was talking, he would ask him whether he didn't know it was rude to interrupt. Questions of the most innocent character he was fond of replying to with a forcible "none-of-your-business," while the same conduct applied to him, he was accustomed to affirm, was of an ungentlemanly character. Grinds on the others he started and pursued with great vigor. Grinds on himself, which were plenty, he was either wont to deny the truth and point of, or endeavor weakly to explain them away, meeting the laughter of the club with a muttered "d—d fools." At first the fellows did not like to get grinds on Jimmy; his fierceness was too much for them. But about the beginning of second term, Senior year, we all began to gain courage. Under the able leadership of Pat Miles, the sceptre was torn away, the glory of Ichabod departed and Stonaker's became a republic where Jimmy took his turn with the rest. The weaker members, who had feared to tackle Jim alone, gained courage with numbers. Jim, whose devotion to the grape, or to the fruit of the hop-vine, sometimes overpowered him, would come down to Sunday lunch a little late. As soon as the club had glanced at him, with one accord they would howl, " Same as I had for breakfast, Sidney," while Jim would take his seat with a look of ineffable disdain on his countenance, and Sidney, the waiter, would produce the tea and toast. The Dog, who thought he knew more French than any one at the table, used to pick Jimmy's French phrases to pieces, about the only thing he could get into Jimmy on. As when Jimmy blew in after Psychology examination and declared that Jimmy's [not Buckelew, but McCosh] grading system was a mere *bagatelle,* or declared that he was positive that all the *demi mode* would be there, etc. From this it may be gathered that at Stonaker's they lived in an atmosphere of grinds. The whole club would pile on one man for a week, and then this unfortunate would join the ranks of the majority, and they would pass on to the next. The Dog got it worst for a time, so much so that he fell into the habit of coming down to meals late, in order to avoid the storm. But he learned to defend himself, and Lesen Sie Foltz and Stallion Smith were the next to suffer.

CLARENCE T. BURGER, C.E., Brooklyn, N. Y.

"Peach" came among us in Sophomore year, with his fair young face, standing like the maiden, "with unwilling feet where the brook and river meet." But Billy Foster captured his affection, and led him away for a time. But soon did "Peach" take back the heart that he gavest him, and join the safe ranks of the Scientif crowd.

FREDERICK WING BURLEIGH, Fitchburg, Mass.

Fred. was one of the prominent figures when we first came on this Campus. He looked so old, and then his white hat and his "See More" coat—never can we forget them! He was not so prominent afterward, for the coat wore out and the hat got smashed, and we got older. But he was well liked, and, noble nature! used to pay his subscriptions to the *Lit.* on time.

PUTNAM CADY, Princeton, N. J.

Cady joined Senior year from Union. He spoke a good speech on Chapel Stage. Further of him the historian knows not.

WILLIAM WHITEFIELD CATOR, Baltimore, Md.

Cator left us at the end of Sophomore year, it was reported to get married. If this was the case his sacrifice was unappreciated. He is still single. Appeared on the Campus the other day in a costume "quite English, you know," and says he shall look in on us at Commencement.

ROBERT E. CARTER, Huntington, L. I.

Carter went into the cane spree with Dunn, '84, and captured his cane. Would that the fight had been by the broad light of noon-day. Would that it had been photographed! A pitched battle between two such mighty warriors would have made a scene worthy of the pencil of Hogarth himself. Carter was called Vermes in Freshman year, and was commonly reported to poll late and be very absent-minded. In fact, so absent-minded that he frequently forgot to wash his face in the morning, and once went without the touch of H_2O for a week. He came up wonderfully afterward, got into the First Division, and tried for the Biological Fellowship.

WARREN B. CHAPIN, New York City.

Chapie was always a lady's man—a man about town. In fact, he was one of the greatest mashers in '85. He prided himself on knowing perfectly how to conduct himself with members of the fair sex. His allegiance was first held by two maidens who dwelt in that district of Princeton which is guarded by the Seminary. That was when he was a crony of the immortal Heady. Later on he left Head and transferred his allegiance to a pretty Hebe who served nectar and ambrosia to the gods who belonged to Mamma Knox's club. Chapie, as we said before, prided himself upon his *savoir faire*, and no slip was ever laid to his charge. But just before going to print the historian received the following letter:

DEAR JOHN:—Chapie recently went to call on a young lady. Arriving at the house about 7:45 P.M., and the young lady being some time in making her appearance, Chip fell asleep on the sofa. His fair hostess finding him there, did not awaken him, but allowed him to sleep calmly on till about eleven, when she shook him up and asked him if "it wasn't about time to go home?"

(Signed) "FACT."

Chapie was very bored about this incident and laid low, but thus was it disclosed. The historian suspects that the note was written by Sherrerd Depue out of revenge for Chapie's having cut him out with the aforesaid fair Hebe.

B

CHARLES STEELE CLARK, Indiana, Pa.

It was never known that any one had ever made an impression on Jingle's hardened heart till Senior year, his time having previously been taken up with playing base-ball and boring little John Dickey. But in Senior year Steele's fate met him. There was a pretty maiden who used to dispense cake and candy to the fellows over the counter at Priest's store. Her Steele saw and loved. Now, Stub Bryan had already made advances in the same direction, having met her at the Nassau rink. Undeterred by his friendship for Stub, Steele resolved perfidiously to undermine him. He went to the restaurant to eat ice cream in the day time, when none would be there, and fancied he was making much progress. But one day when he entered the restaurant, behold! it was not empty, for there were two '86 men there, and inwardly was Steele much bored. And so, when they had all finished, did Steele say to the '86 men, "I will not go yet; I will stay, and I will eat some more cake. Tell them to bring up some cake." And he thought thus to disguise his fell purpose. So the '86 men went down stairs, and they told the maiden to take up some cake to the gentleman, but the maiden refused, and said that she would send the boy up with the cake. Whereat the '86 men went outside, and they called up to Steele, who sat in the window, and they made mock of him, and he went unto the restaurant no more.

ALEX. E. CLERIHEW, Cincinnati, Ohio.

Alec., having a good bass voice, intended to make good use of it when he came to College. To this end after he was elected President of the Class, on George Anderson's ticket, he organized a Freshman glee club, of which he was self-constituted leader, after the fashion of Hiram Gooch in later years. But the University appreciated Alec., and for them he deserted the Class club forever. About the end of Sophomore year Alec. was found to be very anxious about the board at "Ivy" next year, whether "you would get the worth of your money or not," etc. Alas! alas! Alec. never got the chance to see whether "you got the worth of your money or not." His efforts in that line were not appreciated. A sadder and a wiser man he was the next term. He left us at Christmas, Junior year.

JAMES HARLAN CLEVELAND, Augusta, Ky.

"Jim" always wrote his name in full, for the Harlans were mighty men in Gilead when our Class entered College. Yes, Jim was a Harlan, there was no doubt about that; the only doubt in his mind being whether he should rival his relatives on the athletic field or in the class-room. After a struggle he decided in favor of the athletic field, and adorned the Freshman scrub team with his presence. Who does not remember Jim in those days! For he was fresh, very fresh. Peerless Beauty, he was called among the Sophomores, and he wore bright green breeches, with a hole in them, and never cut or brushed his hair. Loud was he on the foot-ball field, loud in maintaining his interpretation of the rules, loud in calling "off side" and "line up." Clumsy in movement, poor in playing, Jim did not make the team; in fact, his success in athletics was not great, with the exception of his forty-five minute fight with Jack Kennedy, in which he secured half the cane. After the fight Jim fainted, and was carried into Jenny's room in East Middle Witherspoon. He was laid upon the sofa, and the remorseful Juniors stood around. "Poor, innocent fellow!" said one, looking at Jim's face, shrouded by his disheveled locks; "Where does he live?" While another produced a bottle of old Bourbon and was proceeding to administer a dose. "Pause," said the first, "we must dilute it. Young and pure as he is, it has never, probably, passed his lips before." "So be it," replied the other, and at that instant, from the sofa was heard a sepulchral voice uttering the fateful words, "I'LL TAKE IT STRAIGHT." Poor, innocent fellow! there was no doubt where he came from. After this Jim gave up athletics and went in for grade, etc. He was a J. O., a Lynde Debater, a Baird Prizeman, and what not. The mantel of the Harlans certainly fell upon him, in this respect at any rate.

JOHN H. CONEY, Cincinnati, O.

"John, you lazy dog!" was a frequent expression among his friends, and it was true. John accomplished about as much, and did about as little work as any man in the Class. John would meet you with a quiet smile when you taxed him with it and say nothing, for he was a self-contained fellow, knew what he was about, and was set in his ways, which were good ones, by the way.

WILLIAM WADDELL CONNER, Washington, Iowa.

It was generally understood that he, Balls, was paying his own way, and the fellows respected him accordingly. His umpiring for the foot-ball team in Senior year was a sight to see. When Balls donned those canvas shoes, that jockey cap, and commenced to use his stentorian voice, he struck terror into the hearts of Yale, and gained from the Harvard papers the epithet of the "sprightly Mr. Connor;" while Birdie was heard to remark that he only hoped they wouldn't take us for a traveling circus.

JOHN S. CONOVER, C.E., Princeton, N. J.

Your bald head will live in my memory, John, for what first drew you to my notice was overhearing a fair damsel say she did wish John Conover would put something on his head to stop the hair from coming out, and she must have intimated this to him, for it was currently reported in the Class that John kept bottles and bottles on his bureau, and spent yearly a small fortune in this line, but to no purpose. Bob Sterry hurt John's feelings severely one day in the Gym. by asking him for a comb. "I have no use for one," said John, with a very red face, and Bowery realized what he had done.

JOHN C. COOPER, Pittsburg, Pa.

Jack was a quiet fellow, who never had much to say to anybody but his cronies, Weir and Jones. He read a good deal, but his passion was base-ball. He played always on our Class Nine, and two years short-stop on the University.

EUGENE C. COULTER, Brockfield, O.

Coulter came among us in Junior year from Williams. He wanted a larger field and pastures new. Williams did not suit him, neither, it was whispered, did he suit Williams. He was called Emperor there, and one of the Williams papers contained a notice that "Emperor Coulter was now honoring Princeton with his presence. May they rejoice more than we did in his patronizing airs." Whenever any one imitated Coulter's pompous voice and manner and called him "Doctah," or "Emperor," Coulter would answer, with cutting severity, "I don't see the application." A reply which invariably caused laughter and disrespect in the aggressor. Coulter met all subscription fiends with calm contempt. He even went so far as to inform one of the *Lit.* men, who was humbly, after his kind, soliciting Coulter's patronage, that he saw no reason why they should exist. A dangerous speech. The freedom of the press must be maintained. It was usually thought that Coulter was of a very innocent and guileless nature. Confirmatory of this belief was his asking of General Kargé whether he would please him best by calling him General, Professor, or Herr, and following up the conversation by begging for permission to use a trans. in Herrmann and Dorothea, "which I have ascertained to be exceedingly difficult of rendering and translation." The General's rage and anguish at this request may be conceived. Nevertheless, the belief in Coulter's purity received a severe shock the day he came down to try how the board was at Stonaker's. Now the fellows at Stonaker's were not desirous of Coulter's company, and, relying on his predilections in favor of standard conversation, resolved, under the leadership of Jimmy Buckelew, whose capabilities in the reverse line were well known, to make it exceedingly unpleasant for the Emperor. They did their best. They greeted the Dog when he came in with such a shower of unpleasant remarks, emphasized in such a forcible manner that he grew exceedingly irate till shown where the Emperor sat munching his food in stiff dignity. If Coulter had come to many meals that club would have lost, every man Jack of them, all hope of future salvation, but they relied on one meal of that description being enough for Coulter's stomach. When, lo! and behold, he called "Griffin," as he named him, outside and informed him that the place suited him and he would like to stay. Unfortunately, there was no room for the Emperor, but thus did Coulter "locate the insect" on Stonaker's club. He scored on them decidedly that time.

MONROE CRAWFORD, Hoboken, N. J.

There was one thing that was never very plain about Crawford, and that was why he didn't leave long ago, if this place was as bad as he made out. "Many a man will go out of this College with bitterness in his heart," he would say, with melodramatic earnestness, which imposed on some credulous souls, like "Huggs," and he opposed the giving of any memorial, " strictly on principle," he said. ' "We don't owe anything to this College. This College hates us. The Faculty hates us. Murray will be glad to see us go. They've never done us any justice. What have we got out of this College? why should we give anything to it?" All of which cranky nonsense Crawford avowed "strictly on principle." The Wreck was fond of fathering the most outrageous opinions upon himself, probably, let us hope, with the object of astonishing his hearers. The effect being, however, often the very opposite. Crawford would argue an absolutely indefensible side with a loud voice and effective manner, because you never could be certain exactly what he would admit and what he wouldn't. He told John Coney once, " Now, you know that a man of my political principles can sway men a great deal better than one of yours, with all your reform and nonsense." This characteristic was very advantageous to the Wreck, but very trying to his antagonist. For we see that the common ground, the common Major Primise of which Jeremy Bentham speaks, could never be obtained.

WILLIAM DARLING, C.E., Wilkesbarre, Pa.

To '84 he adhered as his old class, and '84's historian took him.

AARON DAWES, Hightstown, N. J.

Not from Dawes' Hole or any other part of the sun, but brevet Senator Dawes, you know.

JOSEPH H. DAWSON, Baltimore, Md.

Dawsie left us once for a time [he was on the horn spree], and at the end of Sophomore he departed forever.

SHERRERD DEPUE, Newark, N. J.

Dep. was a quiet and studious boy until in Senior year he began to add a little wildness to his former diligence. It is reportep that he drank so much cider at his club as to fall off his chair, and to cause his father to forbid him anything but H_2O for a week. He paid court to Hebe, in which, as we have before hinted, he got most largely left; and he completely cowed Fred. Wilson by the sharpness of his wit. But, oh! the misery and the mourning of Dep.'s first pipe! Some '86 men fixed it for him, with mild "Lone Jack;" Dep. lit up, and sat by the fire puffing away, feeling as tough as a Turk. Pretty soon Dep. asked them if it was not very hot in the room. On their replying no, he was silent for a time, and then rose and walked uneasily about the apartment, lying down on the sofa at intervals. Finally he insisted that it *was* hot, and he opened the casement, and, with his head out, he gazed at the calm moon, which in her majesty was sailing through the heavens. Dep. was pale for a week after that midnight vigil, and said that the doctor was prescribing *nux vomica*.

JOHN R. DICKEY, Philadelphia, Pa.

Dick lived in mortal terror of the historian, and for two reasons. He knew that the historian *could* give him away, and he knew that he had given the historian cause to give him away. He was fond of riling the historian up by calling him "Dog," and used invariably, rain or shine, to stop outside after recitation, wait until the "Dog" came out, and stoop down and tap his finger on the ground. This was intended to represent the wagging of a dog's tail, and was thought to be a great joke, always provoking great visibility in the perpetrator. When the "Dog" was about to recite, or to make one of his famous and telling speeches in mass-meeting, he was in constant expectation of hearing a yelp proceed from some part of the room, which would give him the grins and cause him to sit down in silent confusion. Dick grew more respectful as it drew towards the end of Senior year. Steele Clark had curried favor with the historian, by teaching him a way to curb Dick's wit, through a gentle use of repartee; and, besides, Dick knew that Nemesis was coming. This repartee consisted in broad allusions to one of Dick's physical characteristics, *i. e.*, his size. Here you had Dick cold. Call him " Runt," and you could shut his box at any moment. After the fellows found out this weakness of Dick's, there was no peace for him. In fact, Steele Clark never called him anything else. And even that meek and lily-like damsel, Poker McIlvaine, found occasion to curb Dick's wit by telling him about a young lady who said she had known all the Ivy men, and, of course, *little John Dickey,* long ago ; also the words "children not admitted," referring to one of Dick's adventures the day he went up to the Yale game, could be used with crushing effect. Another of Dick's physical peculiarities was his eye-sight. This was so bad that Dick was often obliged to keep his glasses on over night that he might see to get up in the morning, despite of Shea's oath and promise that he would remain upon the hearth-rug all night rather than see Dick so put about. But the contrary opinion prevailed. They hung the Jug up by the handle, and they put the pug inside, and they covered him with the shaggy suit, and they laid the pipe near by and left Dick to his peaceful slumbers.

WILLIAM A. DICKEY, Manchester, N. H.

Dick came among us in Junior year, a veritable boomerang of the North, for he too could twist and turn himself in all kinds of ways and directions. It really used to look, when Dick was in the pitcher's box, as if he could even go so far as to return on himself, in the manner of the aforesaid engine of destruction. One day Dick made a home run—on an overthrow of the opposite side ; the manner in which he completed the circuit of the diamond was a marvel to behold, and thenceforward was he known indifferently as Dartmouth, or Rasselas ; reason unknown, but "'twarn't his fault any heaow."

R. J. DODDS.

* * * * * * * * * * * *

NATHAN BROOKE DOLAN, Philadelphia, Pa.

Let us quote a few words from that standard and respectable sheet, the *New York World.* Its estimate of character is excellent, and its essay on " Jolly Boys at College " will be prominent for ages in the history of American literature, as its pictures will be in American art—perhaps. " Dolan, Class of '85, son of Thomas Dolan, the wealthy manufacturer of Philadelphia, lives like a lord, keeps a horse for the saddle, generally enjoys himself without allowing the classics to encroach too much on his time, and depletes the old gentleman's exchequer by something over $3,000 a year." Poor Brooke! if he did come up to the above description, it was not for long. Junior year saw him not with us any longer.

WILLIAM W. DONALDSON, Baltimore, Md.

Tree Toad did not remain with us long. He went away after a year's residence, having so far degenerated as to be seen smoking cigarettes on the Campus in broad day-light. (Old Joke.)

JAMES R. DOUGLAS, Mansfield, O.

* * * * * * * * * * * *

MALVERN N. DUE, Wetumpka, Ala.

The Colonel was a quiet fellow, who talked with a Southern accent, minded his own business, and spent most of his time in his room, smoking and reading. He wrote very well for the *Lit.*, and came near receiving the Contributors' Prize, the judges having some difficulty in deciding.

FRANK T. DUNSHEE, Thompson, Ill.

"H. & D." Dunshee, too, was quiet, worked hard, and debated well in Hall. He entered Junior year and bloomed out at the Hightstown ball, where Wilbur conveyed him, and where he smashed all hearts.

GEORGE B. DURELL, Williamstown, N. J.

George used to be in '83, where he stood very near the top of the Class. He left them in Junior year, taught at Pennington for a time, and played second base in the Pennington Nine in the great game when they defeated '85's Freshman team. He entered '85 in Junior year, resumed, without trouble, his old place near the top, and kept it till the end.

DUNCAN EDWARDS, Brooklyn, N. Y.

If I were a true prophet I should like to write history in advance, and put down the fact that Edwards, the best captain of the Nine in four years, conducted that nine to the championship; but good wishes are all I can give now. Edwards was an Honorman, a J. O., Class Orator, and Captain of the Nine, a good record for one man. His history needs no further enlargement. I have one more hope to offer, which is that he and Doc. Wylie will come through the season both alive. To hear them argue in regard to base-ball affairs you would think that one or the other was in danger of his life.

FRANK G. ELLETT, Laytons, N. J.

Ellett left us for a time, then honored us by his return in Senior year. He took a partial course, fraternized with Lord in Class, and wrote an epic heavy as a stone, which he handed, with great gusto, to an unfortunate *Lit.* man who tackled him for bread in the shape of a subscription.

GEORGE E. ETTER, Harrisburg, Pa.

George entered in Junior year. George belonged to Abe Gaither's crowd. I leave him to his tender mercies, advising him, by the way, never to eat beans for dinner when he expects to go to a chemical lecture in the afternoon.

FREDERICK B. FAITOUTE, Newark, N. J.

Faitoute entered in Junior year from Williams. He purchased an orange-and-black Jersey at once, and played tennis with varying success.

JANON FISHER, C.E., Baltimore, Md.

Fish was a very wise, grave and reverend Senior indeed. It was probably this wisdom and gravity which caused him to be made a tutor in the Scientific School in Senior year. After this he held absolute sway over numbers of unsophisticated Freshmen and Sophomores, who called him Mr. Fisher, and looked upon him with reverence and respect, while our fellows used to bore him intensely by touching our hats to him on the Campus, calling him Professor, and breaking up his dignity by yelling at him when he had his class out on the lawn in front of the Scientif surveying. I have said that Fisher's wisdom was great. I believe that it is; but two incidents have come to my knowledge lately, which rather incline me to believe that even Professor Fish's wisdom can make a slip. Joyful is it that ,the Faculty never heard of them. Perhaps if they had they might have doubted Fish. Nay, as it is, I may be taking the bread and butter from his mouth by relating them, but—truth above all things. Rumor went about that Fish's heart was captivated by a fair maiden who resided in the town of Baltimore, in "Maryland, His Maryland." Be that as it may, Fish attended a ball in the Christmas vacation at which the aforesaid damsel was present. After the approved novel fashion, Fish was unable to get a dance with her the whole evening, and devoured his heart in impatience and jealousy. But he said and did naught, for Fish, it must be understood, was a great society man, the pink of propriety, and prided himself on his *savoir faire*, and his absolute correctness and acquaintance with all matters in the social line. At last Fish saw her alone. The ball-room was comparatively empty. He seized his opportunity, and, rushing up while the music sounded courage in his ears, he begged for a waltz. The damsel looked up at our man of the world and said, with a waggish glance, "Well, really, Mr. Fisher, I'm afraid the music won't suit." And our man of the world, our wise, professional frequenter of ball-rooms, looked at his dancing-card, and ascertained by its aid that they were playing a march. Ah, Fish, Fish! and a member of the Princeton Faculty too! But hear on, for there is more to come. Fish left the ball-room that night crushed after his fearful break, and went away the next day to resume his professional duties, a sadder and a wiser man. But still not wise enough, as ye shall see, for he did not alight at Princeton, but was carried by, and the reason, said he, was that he was thinking abstractly of the fair girl he left behind him, and who had captured his heart; so he got off at Monmouth Junction, and started off at once to walk back that cold winter's night, and, ere he had reached half way, the train from Monmouth passed him, and he, with sorrow and gnashing of teeth, saw it go by. And why had he not been wise enough to wait at Monmouth and ride back in comfort? Because he was thinking abstractly of the fair girl he left behind him, and who had captivated his heart. So he trudged along through the snow, and he reached Princeton Junction, and turned down the track, and kept on his weary tramp, and, ere he had reached half way, the train from Princeton Junction passed him, and a second time he, with weeping and gnashing of teeth, saw a comfortable ride pass by. And why had he not been wise enough to wait at the Junction and ride to Princeton in comfort? Because he was thinking of the fair girl he left behind him, and who had captured his heart. So did Fish make three slips from the path of wisdom in one evening, and I bid him ponder deeply and mend his ways.

JONATHAN C. FOLTZ, Lancaster, Pa.

Foltz entered '85 in Junior year, and what Herr Foltz didn't know was not worth knowing. Marquand's course in art was only what any *respectably well-read* man would know anyhow, and Astronomy was such a snap that Foltz used to spend his time before examination in walking around the Campus of an evening gazing at the stars. So much did Foltz know, in fact, that the fellows at the club used to say he ought to be com pound Professor of Arts and Sciences. One of his numerous nicknames was "Lesen Sie," short for "Lesen Sie was sie geschrieben haben, Herr Foltz," which was the General's favorite exhortation to him when he intended to keep him up for an hour and set him down at the end of it with a "Gott knows you are dumb, Herr Foltz." Sometimes they called him Marks, after the hero of that famous play, "Uncle Tom's Cabin," which drew a larger audience to the University Hall than Clara Louise was able to. "Marks! what will you take? A little gin, if you please," when Foltz was desirous of being helped to anything, was sure to be the cry in chorus. Sometimes they called him Pach, in allusion to his little photographing machine, and sometimes combined the two and called him Pach-Marks. Of word contests he had many with various members of the club, in which, to my mind, he did not come out second best, for Herr

Lesen Sie had a proper sense of his own dignity, and if he thought this had been infringed on, would be distant and cold to the offender for several days. With Ethics Marks was not as conversant as with Astronomy. He, in company with various other youths, received notes from Patton to call at his house. The story of which shall be told hereafter.

JOSEPH C. FOSTER, } Cincinnati, O.
WILLIAM R. FOSTER,

Great twin brethren were they; not of Rome, but of that other classic place, Cincinnatus. Learned, filled with much knowledge they were. First Division men both. Tough were they, tough as the beef-hide of their native plain, and one rowed in the crew that competed for the Childs' Cup. Alike were they, not so alike as Romulus and Remus, whose surname was St. John, yet still well did they resemble each other, and both were in the horn spree; but one escaped, for the other saved him. After they went the way of all flesh, did one come to town and ask after them who said he was their long-lost brother, and men believed him, not because he did not have a strawberry mark on his left arm, but because he was full at the time of asking, and it seemed fit that their brother should be so.

LUTHER W. FROST, C.E., Yonkers, N. Y.

Frosty, often known as Hoar Frost, was the proud composer, in connection with Rod. Wanamaker, of a waltz in Freshman year. They called this waltz after '83, why it is not known, except on the principle, perhaps, on which poor poet chaps dedicate their verses to some noble lord in hopes to gain his powerful patronage. The '83 waltz, however, died a natural death, and Frosty confined his musical efforts thereafter to playing on his jingling piano over in Edwards. Frosty, however, was just like some of those great German composers, as far as they affect great nonchalance in dress. He used to go down to the drawing-room and draw in such a disheveled costume, to use a mild phrase, that the other C. E.'s objected. But, then, carelessness about those little matters is a mark of genius, you know.

ABRAM B. GAITHER, Baltimore, Md.

Brad. was Presentation Orator in Senior year. The fellows got very respectful towards him of whom they had lately made sport, for Brad. was a long, lean, lanky sort of a fellow, who had so many angles you couldn't help getting grinds on him. Now, one would never have suspected Brad. of having any adventures of a romantic nature, but he did; at least he wrote a story for the *Lit.* about his adventures on a steamboat, with a young damsel who occupied the opposite state-room, which was of such an affecting nature, and which the *Lit.* editors, innocent souls though they were, enjoyed so hugely that they nominated him First Alternate on the spot, even though they feared to print the story, it being a little too Practico-Ethical in its contents. Brad. sold a Freshman his room, unfurnished, high up in South-East, for a neat sum, X let us call it. He had hesitated a good deal about putting X on it, fearing it might be too much for the Freshman's pocket. Finding, however, that the Freshman readily acquiesed, Brad. began to repent of his bargain, so he cogitated long and finally went to the Freshman and told him that he was very poor, and that he could not let him have the room for X. "What'll you have?" asked the Freshman. "Four cards," said Brad., out of habit, for he remembered the performances of the old South-East gang, and then he blushed all over his innocent countenance that he should so have incurred the suspicions of his young friend, and corrected himself and said humbly, "It'll have to be $X + 1$." "Very well," said the Freshman, and again did Brad. repent of his bargain and wish he had taxed the Freshman more. So, a few days later, he told his young friend that Jim Stink would certainly have him in jail for debt, unless he got enough for the room to satisfy Jim's demands. "Very well," said the Freshman, "$X + 2$ let it be." And so the process went on in an arithmetical series, like Malthus' subsistence column, till they raised it to $X + 6$, and then Brad. screwed up his courage to screw $X + 7$ out of his young friend, and he went to him, and his young friend told Brad. that he had purchased another room, for "there came a Christian by who was worth a Jewish *buy*," he said.

CAREY B. GAMBLE, Baltimore, Md.

Oh, thou disheveled beauty, thou didst enter in Sophomore year; thou didst play lacrosse. Such was the end of that young man's desire. Carey always had the reputation of leading a sober, righteous and godly life. He kept his peccadiloes dark, if he had any; but once, I am sorry to relate, our friend made a slip from the straight and narrow path. It seems that on Christmas day in Senior year, Carey went out to the Lunatic Asylum, at Baltimore, to pay the lunatics a visit. Why I know not, but as Carey usually did look a good deal like a lunatic when he played lacrosse and his hair fell about his ears, that may be the reason. A touch of nature made him feel akin, perhaps. At any rate, Carey entered the reception chamber, and was hospitably received. After the ceremonies were over, a large bowl of punch was brought in to close the party and make the lunatics remember that Christmas comes but once a year. Of this punch Carey, though not invited, partook so largely, almost to the exclusion of the lunatics, that disastrous consequences followed. The lunatics grew angry at being thus cut out, and Carey, to appease them, said "theywashallgood fellers," and danced a hornpipe for them, and finally walked around the room on his hands. Indeed, his conduct grew so very "merry" that his friend was obliged to hurry him away, lest he be clapped in a straight-jacket and put safely to bed in a cell. Another fact which has come to my knowledge about Carey, leads me to believe that his knowledge of Scripture was not very extensive; and my reason for such belief is that I have heard that when Carey was put the pertinent question, "Where was Moses when the light went out?" he did not know. Be that as it may, it is certain that to the analogous question, "What was Carey doing when the light went out?" he only replied, "Oh! oh! oh!"

B. A. GASKELL, Mt. Holly, N. J.

* * * * * * * * * * * *

PERSIFOR F. GIBSON, B.S., Philadelphia, Pa.

Gibby-Tree, often known in Fresh. year as Goose Gibby, was not as "handsome as Tree-Gibby, but he was just as dog." He set the fashions for us for four years, and was a member of the

Cabinet in Senior year. It is said that Gibby never lost his
dignity, but he was the victim, in Fresh year, of a joke played
upon him by Coyle, '84, which caused Gibby to use profane
words, and Hermann Huss to dismiss the class because "some-
tings must have died in dot room." I forbear to mention more,
but a few words about our relations with Coyle may not be in-
appropriate. Coyle was a Fresh Soph., who roomed in University Hall among numerous Freshmen. So numerous were
we that we used to reverse the regular order of things and haze,
instead of being hazed. We plagued Coyle in all sorts of fashions, and finally, with the aid of Gibby's long pipe, we smoked
him out. He rose in his wrath and appeared at his door, pistol
in hand, and told us, in unmistakable terms, that he would
shoot some of us if we didn't look out, emphasizing his threat
with a variety of strange oaths, in the use of which he was pro-
ficient. At that moment a pitcher of water was poured over
him from behind, kindling still further his anger, but effectually
extinguishing his powder. In revenge he played the trick on
Gibby to which I have alluded above. The trick was quite in
keeping with Coyle's character, which was not particularly high,
as the following fact will signify. A lady friend of Coyle's was
visiting him at Princeton. Several students came to call in the
evening and they fell into a discussion on College nick-names.
"I do think they are so appropriate," said the lady-friend;
"it's wonderful how students hit off each other's character in
that way. What's your name, Andrew?" Andrew hesitated;
he looked at the others, eager to tell the lady friend if he
should falsify the truth, and, with blushes suffusing his handsome features, he replied, "Guiteau." Tableau.

HENRY W. GLEDHILL, Paterson, N. J.

Kid's performances on our foot-ball team in Fresh year
were notable. He used to play "Back" because he could kick,
the fellows said—and so he could—at the Captain, at the
directors; but at the ball, ah! that was another matter. Kid
also was very prominent the night of the horn-spree. He nearly
became involved in a fight with Scotty, by taxing him with
being under the influence, but friends kept them apart, as shall
be told hereafter.

HIRAM GOOCH, Louisville, Ky.

Poor Hiram was a little deaf, and couldn't see why the fellows should put upon him on that account. As when Charley Shields would be about to call somebody up and every one would cough, so that Hiram couldn't hear, and then shout, "Hiram ! Hiram !" Hiram would rise wonderingly, looking at Charley. Mutual explanations and apologies would then be entered into by these too polite gentlemen, and Hiram would sit twirling his mighty mustache in rage. Despite this deafness, Hiram was a great musician, and tried every year, like Billy Scott and Nancy Lee, for the Glee Club. Finding this of no avail, he founded a little private glee club, of which he was *ex-officio* the leader. But even this did not succeed. The fates seemed against Hiram. All the members of this little glee club resigned, and formed another one, of which Hiram was not a member. The "Nightingale" was dumb after that slight; he confined himself to the zithern's melodious notes. But Hiram had fulfilled another function. It must be confessed that in Freshman year Hiram was a bit of a Shylock. He used to buy and sell rooms on commission; but once, when he came to secure a room for himself, was the biter bit. He paid $150 for a $75 room, and, to quote the *Princetonian* of that date, "when taxed with the extravagance, he replied that he had been brought up in the greatest luxury; but was seen eating peas with his knife the next day at Dohm's."

TEVIS GOODLOE, Louisville, Ky.

Tevis left us at the end of Freshman year, and went to Williams. Was universally regretted.

JOHN L. GRAHAM, New York City.

"A good man to have along on a starry night; money in abundance, and rated among the bloods as a spender," to quote the interesting article in the *New York World* again. Yes, the "Dog," as he used to be called, was certainly a spender. He could draw the long bow pretty effectually, too, at times. He loved and lost that Emma who put him in such a dilemma.

c

He did not love his books, but he lost them likewise. Second term, Junior year, saw him no longer with us. He went to China—not to fight the French.

WILLIAM L. GRANBERY, Columbia, Tenn.

"Granny" was one of the warmest and kindest-hearted fellows in '85. In athletics he came out wonderfully Sophomore year. But, alas! alas! Granny bet all the money he had in the world on Birdie's crew in the race at Philadelphia, with the usual result. Preferring to keep on South, where the roads were drier and the walking better, Granny left us, and never came back.

WILLIAM J. GREENE, C.E., Cedar Rapids, Ia.

It was not hard to bore the good old man, or Fayther, as we used to call him, he took everything so seriously, and was so sober and sedate about everything. This, however, did not prevent his making a trial of all the acids in the laboratory to see which one suited his drunkard's palate best. Fayther would come down to the club smacking his lips over some ammonia or acetic undilute which he had just drunk, and eat a big dinner on the strength of it. As I said before, Fayther was easily worked up. I kept him on pins and needles for a month about some grind, which, I informed him, I had secured. He would beseech me to tell him in vain, and would always wind up with a pathetic "Well, if Miles told it to you, you can be sure it isn't true." The fact of the matter was that the only grinds there were on Fayther was the story about his saying that there would be a *polytechnic* display the night of the election, and the other story of how he said he used to call every Sunday night somewhere, and how they always sang hymns, and, after that, they sang *sexual* songs. Fayther always denied the truth of these tales, but I fear me, Fayther, they are true. Perhaps Fayther's brain had become clouded by too much frequenting the "Lafayette." Who knows?

FRANK M. GRIFFITH, Jacksonville, Ill.

Griff. was always a prominent youth, from the time when, in the autumn of '81, he first bloomed among us, a veritable cornstalk from the West, for his pervading tint was yellow. Indeed he was so yellow that when he went with the Democratic campaign corps to Trenton, in Senior year, the boys in the streets all saluted him as the cheese-headed dude. Griff. played second base on our Class Nine in the fall of Fresh year, and that was what brought him first under our notice; that is, he played for a little while. How he played, I forbear to mention; suffice it to say, that in our game with '82, Jim Rafferty instructed his men, after the first inning, in a very audible voice, not to try to make base-hits, but "to bat 'em down, good and easy, to second base, and you'll make your first every time." Griff. ceased from athletics after that stab, until in Senior year he appeared on the foot-ball field, as a candidate for the scrub. Here, too, Griff. was unsuccessful or unfortunate. He was in the habit of taking occasional somersets over Tilly Lamar's back, in a fashion that was wonderful to behold, whenever he attempted to tackle that nimble gentleman. But Griff. persevered till he hurt his knee, and closed his athletic career. To see and hear Griff. now, one would never imagine that he had ever been affected with the verdancy of Freshman year. Now he has a contempt for innocence and freshness which is most edifying to contemplate. You can't teach Griff. anything. He knows the ropes. He's been through it all, and his lack of reverence for constituted and collegiate authority is most refreshing to any one who has fears of the powers that be. How often has Griff. condemned these fears when expressed, yet the fact remains that there are strange contradictions in Griff's nature. In Freshman year, one balmy night of early autumn, Griff. and Halsey had been over in town, with what fell purpose I know not, but I suspect cream punch. They were wending their way across the deserted Campus, and they wondered what their mothers would have thought if they had known that they were out at such an hour, and they felt guilty and the cold air of night struck them and they hastened, when, oh, horror! the great bell in North began to toll, toll as if it never would stop, and they knew that it was nine o'clock, and they not in their rooms, with their lights out, as the College laws, which they kept carefully in their pockets next their hearts, required, and they hastened still more, but ere they had reached mid-campus they saw a tall figure approaching, muttering to itself, and they knew that it was Jimmy, and great fear fell upon them, and they thought of expulsion and disgrace, and almost shrieked in their anguish; and Griff., in an agonized whisper, said to Steve, "Let us hide behind yon tree," and they did so, and Jimmy passed by and saw them not, or if he did took no heed. But Griff., alas, has lost that pristine innocence of his, never to to be gained again. Now doth he delight in late hours and all that he should not. His meat and drink are grinds—on others, not himself, though these last are numerous, such as those of which the Dog of Venice and the Post Graduate (P. G.) who drew that picture in the *Bric-à-Brac*, can probably inform you better than I. Another of Griff.'s distinguishing characteristics was his unwillingness ever to let a chance slip. He believed in taking everything you could get, and having no waste. There was a story current about Griff. which illustrates this point, even though not strictly true, perhaps, in every particular. He was walking along Sixth Avenue one day, in company with McAlpine, when, all of a sudden, a large and unusual sign on the other side of the street—

TRAMPS WANTED TO EAT UP THE FREE LUNCH.

Ah, there, my size!" cried Griff. in delight, and he made one dive across the street.

"Griff., where's the bar?" "Oh, it's in there, playing cards." But of course you were perfectly straight that day, going up on the boat to the Yale game, wern't you, Griff.?

WILLIAM HALL, Bedford, Pa.

Most exasperating sort of fellow Billy was. No grinds on him at all. The only thing he did out of the common was to be one of the unfortunate *non vult* crowd, and that wasn't a joke—quite the reverse. But then, on the other hand, it was nice to have Pillee around when the fellows were boring you; for he never saw the joke. He remembered it, however, and used to carry it over home with him in a paper parcel, put it under his pillow, cogitate over it long and deeply, "catch on" about two in the morning, laugh a loud ha, ha! and commence to rub it in after perhaps three days' mature reflection. Billy was Treasurer of the Base-Ball Association, and of the *Lit.* for a time, and proved himself an efficient business man in both positions.

C. T. D. HALSEY, Newark, N. J.

A society life wearied Steve's brain, and he left us for a rest. He is now running '86, and to the tender mercies of the '86 historian do I commit him.

ALEX. HARDCASTLE, Goldsboro, Md.

Poor Hardie was always laboring under some physical infirmity, so much so that the fellows got quite callous to his harms. He left '83 on account of his eyes. He used to be away about half the time from our Class for the same reason. And on the foot-ball field! Hardie would give his famous leap preparatory to making a run. Down he would come. "Oh! Hardcastle hurt again. Go ahead." In fact, just before the Pennsylvania-Sophomore game, Kid Toler observed, in cutting accents, " Now, Hardcastle, play on the ground no wings to-day, please!" and Hardie obeyed, and, for a wonder, was not hurt. He did not graduate, but left at the end of Junior year.

J. BORDEN HARRIMAN, New York City.

Bord. was one of those kind of men whom the lady spectators always think play the best. "Oh, who is that? I do so want him to win. What a beautiful complexion!" etc. One of those pretty boys, in fact. Still Bord. was a good athlete. He usually did manage to win, to please the young ladies. He was so polite, you know. Of a truth, Bord. was a graceful youth, but 'twas surprising, nevertheless, how he sometimes would manage to knock the bar off when his body had got apparently safely over. Insolent youngsters in the gym. used to ask sometimes for a ride behind, but of that enough. Bord. was not one of these excessive men, by any means. He usually went in moderately for everything. He went in for athletics—running, jumping and foot-ball alike. And he went in for polling a little—a very little. And he went in for other things which shall be nameless, a little. Who does not remember Bord's air when, with great delight, he would declare that he had had an S. L. the night before, and was still feeling the effects. "S. L." being a symbolic representation of the meaning that Bord. had been "very merry" the night before on the strength of having passed Physics or some such important achievement. G. L., which meant *Heavy Burden*, was reserved for great occasions like an engagement, etc. Keep it up, Bord., old fel. *Ut nequid nimis* is a good motto, and Bord. held by it pretty faithfully but in one respect. Mouse-hunting was his passion. It was the very air he breathed. And after a long chase did he capture a mouse, it did not capture him he said. Soon it grew tame, pretty creature! and would not leave him, but desired to eat out of his hand, and after he had played with it a while our cruel Lothario grew fickle. "Oh, you are too hard on us New York girls, Mr. Harriman," and did not care for the pretty creature any more. And Bord. was much bored with it, and feared lest the Presentation Orator might give him a mouse-trap with a piece of cheese in it to make mock of him, but whether Brad. Gaither will do so or not does not appear at this time of writing.

JOHN M. HARRIS, Taylorsville, Pa.

A man of consuming ambition, that ate away his heart, was John; for his ambition was not satisfied. Verily, a glorious Ivy Orator would he have made, or a fine and cutting Censor. Even the Class-Day Committee might have been honored by his presence, but, like Sisyphus in Lucretius, "he sought the fasces and the sharp axes from the people, and always beaten and sad retires." Never mind, John, there is a future for you yet, when you publish that essay on Matthew Arnold and Celtic Literature you have had in mind so long.

JAMES E. HAYES, Princeton, N. J.

Hayes was a First Division man, but also took an interest in outside affairs, played base-ball and was on the Class Nine, two traits which, when combined, always gain esteem for a man from the majority of the Class.

WALTER B. HEAD, Allegheny City, Pa.

Poor Heady left us not long ago, having pretty thoroughly sacked the University of all that was portable, in the interior of two trunks, and having borrowed enough of the inhabitants, in the way of shekels and other necessaries, to keep him for a time. The Freshmen will miss his patronage. Pity not to have kept him here as a sort of under-tutor, that he might continue to instruct incoming classes through the long years in the mystery of mixed drinks.

CHARLES A. HEALEY, C.E., Atalanta, Ga.

Jack was a Southerner. A Southerner of pronounced type, and he had all the Southern characteristics, among others, that of an extremely high temper, which was what, in the end, got him into difficulty. First term, Junior year, Jack was walking down by the canal, and perceived a rabbit running by, evidently in great haste. Jack picked up a stone and was lucky enough to settle that rabbit's hash forever and a day. Suddenly up came a couple of snobs, with a dog, and claimed the rabbit as theirs, for they had been chasing it. Jack, of course, refused to give up his prize; the snobs grew very insolent, and, though it was two to one, Jack gave them battle. He hit one with a brick over the head, and scared the other so that he ran away. But it proved that the fellow's skull was injured, and it was thought he would die, so Jack fled the town. The man did not die, but Jack did not come back. He went to Stevens, where he satiated his desire for gore by playing on the Stevens foot-ball team.

C. T. HOOD, Sparta, Ill.

Hood did not stay here long. A maiden had captured his affections, and he went West and married her, and they entered the University of Michigan together and may be there yet.

M. Z. HITTEL, Colebrookdale, Pa.

Hittel also faded soon away. We remember him as having made a supreme effort against that dollar-devouring curse, the mortar board. His speech in class-meeting was a great one.

JAMES R. HUGHES, Bellefonte, Pa.

Hugs was one of our business chaps. Sold rooms on commission to Freshmen. Whether he roped 'em or not ask of them. Hugs was also a member of the Pennsylvania militia, I'd have you know, and must be handled with becoming respect lest we offend against that bulwark of the Union, the National Guard.

JAMES L. HUMPHREY, New York City.

"Bones, you fat rascal," they used to call him, and those who have seen him will appreciate the wit and the reason thereof. In Bones we see well illustrated that principle of philology which declares that one word may be developed out of another with a kindred root. For Bones was first a Poller. Then did he take lessons in the Princeton dancing class, and we see, as Granny Hunt says, the formation of the word Po(l)ka. From thence did Bones fall into bad company. He knew those in the class whom he should not have known, and we have the Semitico-Aryan Po(l)ker. Yes, such was the development. And Bones tried to keep up each line symmetrically. Polk would he in the afternoon. Poke would he to the wee small hours. Poll would he afterward, when those wee small hours were growing larger. But it was too much for Bones. He grew thinner and thinner, and finally faded away like a mist from our midst.

JOHN G. JENNINGS, Brady's Bend, Pa.

Jennings has no history connected with '85. He came, he stayed a month, he went silently as he came.

WILLIAM F. JACKSON, Newark, N. J.

Jack was one of those omniscient, omnipresent men who come to College with great expectations on every point. Indeed, I am not sure he did not, like Buz Kempshall, expect to stand first in the class. Yes, Jack was an exuberant youth. He polled much at first, and was so delighted when he got into the First Division that he sent home a telegram at once. He also aspired to athletic fame, went into the cane spree, but lost his cane in thirty seconds to Jay Finney. He tried foot-ball, and when

Jack appeared in his blue-and-white sleeveless Jersey and his tremendous legs we all thought Jack would be a holy tear. But all the tear Jack made was to tear his clothes. He did not make the class team, and showed a commendable gentleness towards Judge Lawton, Kid Toler, or any of those men when they started on a run. Still, he got a substitute's place on the strength of those legs, which a pair of orange-and-black stockings set off to great advantage, and which Jack prided himself on as the apple of his eye. He went over to Pennington when the team went over, but was observed to pay more attention to the fair boarding-school damsels, who sat on the fence, and who greatly admired Jack, than he did to the game. Jack curbed the Sophomores, when they yelled Fresh. at him, by retorting, " Soph., Soph.," in a very nasal tone, as much like theirs as possible. He gave a splendid spread in Fresh. year, and thereby gained the eternal gratitude of all who attended it; for it was fine, there was no doubt about that. But Jack soon deserted polling and athletics for business. Jack was emphatically *the* business man of our Class. What he didn't know about finance wasn't worth knowing. He was business manager of everything that had any such department. Ran the *Bric-à-Brac*, &c., &c., but also had a keen look-out for his own pocket all the while. No flies about Jack in that respect. It used to be quite a joke to say tha " Jackson, '85, was in town last week," as they do in the *Princetonian*, for Jack was always away; he owned a free pass on the railroad, be it understood. What took Jack away so much no one knew, though it was suspected that an *affaire de cœur* had something to do with it. Hush ! let us go no further.

JOHN E. JOHNSON, New York City.

Johnny was a member of that dissipated club Van Dyne's. He, too, like John Coney and Psyche Depue, was overcome—by the cider; for Johnny was an innocent boy, and knew not wine. Now, it is usually the case that when one one gets " very merry " after this fashion one gets also very talkative. But the reverse was the case with Johnny; for the first was his natural state, and he grew silent, which was his unnatural state. Verily he could keep up a clatter, but one could calm him down when one called him Admiral Foote; for his feet *were* large, and he knew it.

HENRY K. JONES, Fortress Monroe, Va.

Jones, thou cynic, thou hypercritical youth, companion of P. Weir; who lovedst much the chase, in which thou rarely didst succeed, being as unlucky in that respect as our respected Thorpey. Jones, never did I think that aught could touch thy heart, till I heard Cooper, with great glee, tell a tale of how thou madest frequent calls on a damsel here in town. And wert observed to grow moody and sad, and not thine own joyous self; and one night thou camest into Cooper's room late at night, and sat by the fire after the approved melodramatic fashion, and with thy head on thy hand, and Cooper asked thee what ailed thee, and thou didst reply with feverish earnestness, "I wonder whether she really loves me?" Farewell, Jones; I leave thee to puzzle it out.

ALFORD KELLEY, Baltimore, Md.

Kelley was in our Class a short time, then went away, and later on joined '86.

EATON M. KEMPSHALL, Elizabeth, N. J.

Buzzy was one of those youths on whom the beneficent effect of a college course is very plain. Buz became much better after he entered College. From being a jaded, worn-out man of the world he became again a fresh, innocent youth, and consorted chiefly with members of the Philadelphian *K. T. λ*. But the gift of gab he never lost. Verily well was he named Buz; for he could buz loud and strong. Gall also was another characteristic which Buz never parted with. After selling the room in which he roomed along with that reverend saint, Pard Lamberton, to a Freshman in Senior year, he felt unlike the fowls of the air, and had nowhere to lay his head; so he quoth unto Charley Van Ausdal, who was of a good-natured turn, "Charley, I'm coming up to room with you," and proceeded to carry his threat into execution at once. Charley heard with inward anguish, but, being of a weak and guileless heart, offered no resistance. Now, after this arrangement was consummated, Buz felt the need quite often of a pleasant apartment where he and his friends could meet together of an afternoon and make patchwork quilts for the heathen. So he cast about in his mind, and he found that the Freshman who had bought his room was in the habit of being out in the afternoon. So Buzzy did invite his friends, and they went to the Freshman's room, and did open the door by force, and did spend their afternoons in great ease and comfort, and did burn the Freshman's coal and smoke his choice tobacco; but one afternoon they left some of their patchwork behind them, and the Freshman saw it and was wrothy, and had a new lock put on his door, and stopped their fun for that time. Buzzy, in company with several other unfortunates, such as Urquhart, Foltz, Gooch, A. Smith, Lord and others, received one of the bogus conditions gotten out in Patton's name in Senior year. Great was the sorrow, but not so the surprise, when these notes were received; for the Ethics examination had caused much fear. Buzzy went down among the first to Patton's house, but after the second man had appeared Patton had "caught on," and amused himself by playing with his fish a little. His dialogue with Buzzy, as reported, may serve as a type of the rest. " Did you get my note?" said Patton out of the corner of his mouth, through his nose, and with a twinkle in his eye—sure sign of mischief. "Yes, sir," said Buzzy. "Why didn't you come before?" Buzzy explained humbly that he had been out of town and had not received the note till lately. "Were you surprised?" said Patton. Buzzy hemmed and hawed and got red, and finally admitted that he wasn't very much surprised. " Did you try hard?" Buzzy protested by all the gods in heaven that he hadn't slept for three days before the examination. " Did you think you'd get through?" asked Patton. Buzzy declared that such had been his conviction, and wept inwardly to think of his mistake. "Well," said Patton, " you're correct in your surmise, Mr. Kempshall, and the principle of egoistic hedonism gives me pleasure in handing you your paper marked up to the absolute norm of an even fifty." Buzzy wept again, but this time for joy.

WILLIAM S. KITTLE, San Francisco, Cal.

Kittle was a great, tall, lanky fellow, who could punt a foot-ball pretty well, and had been a member of the Lawrenceville team. On the strength of the above facts he was elected captain of the

Class foot-ball team in our first class-meeting, but was soon afterwards politely requested to resign, which he did, and so bowed out of the athletic field forever. He and Thorpey used to be great men for going off on long shooting expeditions, from which they would return triumpant, having secured one woodchuck or something of the kind. Kit left us at the end of Sophomore year, and is now hunting prairie dogs in his Western wilds.

SANFORD N. KNAPP, Peekskill, N. Y.

Knapp was one of those men who kept very quiet the first two years of the course. Yes, Knapp laid low and polled much, but in Junior year he blossomed out like the bud into the rose, to use a poetical comparison. Indeed he became a gay gallant and "a lordly villian," too, for down with him, along the broad road, did he lead poor innocent Beattie, as we have before hinted, but only for a time. One afternoon, after dinner, before Reunion, great was the assemblage as usual. But all were quiet. All felt as if some mighty portent were in the sky, and the hush and horror of expectation was there, and a shadow hung over each. No foot-ball was kicked, no base-ball was thrown, no lacrosse stick twined itself in the legs of the unwary passer-by, and suddenly out of West they saw come stealing a figure. Hold thy breath, reader, 'twas a Corpse, and a living Corpse; and on its wasted shape a dress-suit clung, and on its arm a spring coat hung that the dress-suit might not be hid, and on its skull it carried a plug hat. Round the corner of the building it stole, and it blushed a fiery red, and they knew who it was, and then, of a truth,

> There was shouting 'mong men of the Reunion gang,
> Fosters, Jacksons, Johnsons, they rode and they ran.

For not Young Lochinvar, but Young Knapp had come out of the West. "Heads out!" was at once the shout, and so they followed him to the station, and Knapp was secretly well pleased. And he carried off his "fair Ellen," who was Beattie, safely, for he found him waiting at the station, not attired in a dress-coat, but in a nice black suit and a red tie. And where were these two youths bound? Ah, it had occurred to the fertile mind of Knapp that all the other dudes were going to the opera now, and that therefore he must not "go back on his crowd," as the saying is, so he persuaded Beattie to go with him, and they went to New York. And of course it was the correct thing to wear a dress-suit, and why not let the fellows have the pleasure of seeing it while he was about it? Very kind, I'm sure, but hear ye the rest of this true tale. After the opera was over of course it was the correct thing to go to Delmonico's for supper, and, oh, horror! Knapp ordered up the fruit of the vine, the juice of the grape. But here rose Beattie's virtuous soul, and he turned away his eyes, and would not look on the serpent when it was red, but Knapp did, and he finished it. Knapp was an Emersonian sort of a chap, too. He said once that he thought he should have to go on the *Lit.* for the honor of Old Whig Hall, as only two were trying from there. And he bought a set of Emerson's works, and did write an esssay thereupon, but it glided away, after weeping and gnashing of teeth of the editors, into the basket which holds the waste. And, finding that it proved of no avail, he had a dream. Ye Gods! what a dream. About how he was wheeling through a green valley, and got down to rest, and fell asleep, and lovely maidens visited him, and how he awoke. And he handed that into the *Lit.*, but that, too, caused weeping and gnashing of teeth, and the editors felt like Joseph's brethren, and desired to kill Knapp, and, when it was not printed, Knapp's heart grew cold, and he wrote no more for the *Lit.* But he remembered the dream, and he copied it out, and he sent it to four of his lady loves in succession that they might admire it. For Knapp was a lady's man, and used to declare that he knew no pleasanter time than those days when he used to float in a boat—not a canal boat—down the Hudson river, and read Emerson to the fair girl at his side.

CHARLES R. KNOX, Bloomfield, N. J.

Motherly wert thou in appearance. Motherly, kind at heart wert thou, oh, Mamma; and thy club called themselves Mamma's Darlings, and were glad. With charity towards all, with malice towards none, didst thou pass thy course, universally liked and respected.

HENRY LAMBERTON, Winona, Minn.

The first time I ever saw Pard. was in recitation, once when the First and Second Divisions recited together. Yes, actually, Pard. was in the Second Division then, and Billy Sloan saw him, half asleep in the corner, as usual, and called out, "You, you, you there in the corner. What's your name? Get up and recite." Pard. woke slowly and rose still more slowly, unfolding himself gradually, like a boa-constrictor from his folds, and after he had arrived at his full height, he put both hands in his pockets, then he took a little while to think, and finally, with dignity, drawled out in his deep bass voice, "My name's Lamberton, sir," and sat down. Meantime, Billy was nearly consumed with impatience, and the class with laughter, while this was going on. I never forgot that scene, it remains a picture to this day. And of that character was Pard. ever after; I never saw him but I think he was half asleep.

R. S. LAWRENCE, Wichita, Kan.

Lawrence passed his College days with his heart enthralled by some Western maiden. It may be it was that which made him cranky at times. "Touch me with care," was written all over him then, and he thought our Class was the meanest Class in College, and when you taxed him with thinking so, he would stutter with rage and call out, "You can just shut up," and he wanted to swear, I have no doubt, but was too good.

WILLIAM LAWTON, Jr., Kingston, N. Y.

Lawton was a fine foot-ball player, and captained our Freshman foot-ball team as no team has been handled since. He was very popular and was much regretted when he went away, at the end of Sophomore year.

S. HARPER LEEPER, Jr., Frankfort Springs, Pa.

I was walking up the street with Charley once, and asked him for some grinds on himself. He said, with an air of great annoyance, "Why, I would with the greatest amount of pleasure, but I've left 'em up in my room." Under this figurative statement you may learn the rest. " Got a cigar, Charley ? ", some one would say as Charley was lighting up, after dinner. "Why, confound it," he would reply, "this is my last one; I left the others up in my room." Poor Charley, they did used to bore him so down at his club; I will leave him alone. *Quantum sufficit*, as I have said before.

JOHN C. LORD, Morristown, N. J.

Oh, thou pink of purity, propriety and precision! Thou who alone comest up to Granny's three canons of the writer's art in thy behavior! Fain would I handle thee with gloved hands, but 'tis the nature of my office not. Truly, a blighted being wast thou. In thy case virtue did not get its reward. Gladly would'st thou have passed thy days in the high Episcopalian church, but recitations forbid. Gladly wouldst thou at least have passed thy Sundays there,.but that even here a cruel Presbyterian parent forbid. Still didst thou struggle against fate nobly; thou didst go to Chapel on Sundays, but also didst thou rise early, and attend what thou calledst Matins, also, Even Song; also, Prime, perhaps, and Vespers. All these didst thou frequent; for thou wast high, high of a highness. Once, when the Presbyterians held their Luther Celebration here, did one ask thee whether thou wert about to attend, and thou didst answer, with reverend, pained and astonished look, " Can I go to honor him of whom I can ne'er forget that he introduced schism into the Church?" Ah, Lord, I could prophesy of thee that into a nunnery, I mean a monastery, thou wouldst hie thee, were't not that thou likest the female sex too well, and art in the habit of making calls upon gentle dames, which last, in the average, about six hours. Or, perhaps, thou art a gentle dame thyself, in disguise, who knows?

WILLIAM H. LYNCH, Fairhill, Md.

Yes, we remember thee, Oh, Lynch! by thy twangs and thy quiet ways. But beware of sliding on the ice. Beware! lest we have thee no longer to remember.

D. HUNTER McALPINE, New York City.

Mac attended our first class-meeting in full athletic costume, knickerbockers, blue-and-white Jersey, &c., &c., and, what is more, he had a foot-ball under his arm. When the President, Alec. Clerihew, said, " The election of foot-ball captain is now in order," Mac arose, in all his glory, and slung the foot-ball across the room to Billy Hall. I had not seen Mac till then, and he made a deep impression on my mind. He must be a great athlete, I thought, and decided that he was my man for captain—none other. But alas! Mac was balked in this, and the immortal Kittle gained the suffrages of the Class. Mac got on the team and played End Rush, making the famous run-in and touch-down which gave us the lead on the Pennsylvania Freshmen. Mac was honored with a place on the Sophomore Proc., being known as Monkey McAlpine in those days, and got on the Glee Club in our Sophomore year. From that time on Mac had his fill of the management for which his soul longed, Chairman of the Reception Committee, Leader of the Glee Club, and what not. All of which he carried through with success, if with an imperial hand. In Senior year, after the Glee Club concert in Louisville, Mac met with quite a serious accident. He hurt his face quite severely, there being a round red spot upon it about the size of a silver dollar. Now, the peculiar thing about this was that whenever you commiserated Mac, or asked how it had occurred, or even in joke addressed him as Scar-face, he never took this sympathy or badinage kindly, but always blushed, and proceeded to explain irately and with great earnestness, that *he had fallen against the scenes*, that's all.

CHARLES F. McCLUMPHA, Amsterdam, N. Y.

Chumpy, perhaps I should rather say Miss Chumpy, for he was of a feminine character and habits, used to defy me to get any other grinds on him except that one about his constantly falling asleep. And I believe he was right. He used to fall asleep at all times and places, some of them of a most shocking though *feminine* description. Even under the awful eye of Brackett he would doze away. He would fall asleep even when he was reading aloud, even on the very point of beginning, as when he started to give us some poetry and read out, in the most solemn, pathetic tone, "What is he doing, the great dog Pan?" If any one read to him he was sure to be interrupted in the midst of the most affecting portion by a loud snore, which completely destroyed the illusion. If you were in the next room and heard a loud crash, never fear. It would prove to be only Chumpy in a heap on the floor, his books around him, and wrapped in the arms of Orpheus, as the Freshman said. When Chumpy, however, was awake, he was of a most feminine and vivacious character. If he saw anything which surprised him he would give a little squeal, so cunning that it made you feel like clasping him in your arms for protection. At other times he was more vivacious than feminine and developed such a capability for giving the fair Hebe at Van Dyne's the grins by his wit that she told Chapin if Mr. McClumpha didn't stop his behaviour the club couldn't stay there any longer. Ah! Chumpy, Chumpy, little did I think it of thee till I heard it confirmed by the unsullied lips of Cleveland himself [Jim, not Grover]. Ah! I fear that soon wilt thou fall away from thy pristine innocence. Did I not hear thee declare once that when thou wentest to Germany thou wouldst be Bohemian and disrespectable! *O tempora! O mores!*

JAMES L. McCORMICK, Bel Air, Md.

* * * * * * * * * * * *

JOHN B. McFERRAN, Louisville, Ky.

John was a masher. Great impression did he make on many hearts as he stood in the front row of the Glee Club and sweetly warbled a few warbs. In fact, one might almost say that John was irresistible. An incident which happened to him in Senior year confirmed him for the time in this belief. Oh, that fatal, fatal accident to his knee, which was the cause of one of the greatest disappointments of his life! When the Glee Club sang in Philadelphia John was unable to sing, as he was laid up with his knee, and they took Jack Calhoun with them in his place. Soon afterwards John received a letter from two fair damsels whom Alfy Baker and Bunny Spencer declared they knew, and who were in the habit of calling Alfy "Darling Bob" and Bunny "Their own Wabbit," in sportive jest. This letter contained some expressions which pleased John mightily, and others which he could not understand. Of the first character they declared they would love him forever; that they were not summer friends, but would retain the warmth of their affection even through the cold of winter; that his beauty and his warbling (not in the technical sense of the word), had gone to their hearts, etc. But what did they mean by saying that they admired his stalwart form and manly proportions (for John was small of stature); and what did they mean by pitying him for not being able to raise a mustache, when the one which John possessed was his joy and pride? John investigated. No wise proceeding, John; for where ignorance is bliss, etc. Oh, horror! It was not he they meant; him they ignored; him they thought not of; him they never knew or saw. It was Jack Calhoun who had captured their affection. Poor John!

CLARENCE W. McILVAINE, St. Albans, Vt.

If one were to follow Poke's course from its very beginning one would see him on the train which conveyed numerous young aspirants towards the goal of their ambition—the position and dignity of a Princeton undergraduate. One would have seen him walking up and down the train, a white traveling-cap upon his head and his straw hat carefully hung upon a peg, and one would have marked a look of anxious agony upon his countenance, a look as if he could have wept, a look as if mighty thoughts were surging through his mind. And they were— thoughts of the morrow's examinations. That look reminded one of the look one sees in the General's noble visage, when an unfortunate youth makes a slip in an irregular verb. And that look was deeper and deeper impressed upon his brow the next day, and care and woe so weighed upon his mind that it went astray, and he got rattled in Baby Rockwood's examination; and McIlvaine—yes, McIlvaine—the great McIlvaine failed to pass. And the anguish of those days was not soon over, and it had driven all other thoughts and memories from his mind, it seemed; for on the morrow, when we were all at the Junction jubilant at being through, and when two trains were approaching, one from either hand, I marked again that look of woe on Poker's brow, and then I saw courage flash into his eye and he took resolution and humbly approached a mighty man, whom he thought was a Senior, but who was only a Freshman and asked him with becoming respect, " Please, sir, can you tell me which way the train goes to New York?" If we look at the next stage in Poker's career we should see him at a club in Witherspoon street with his bosom friend Scharff. Talk with Scharff ten minutes and he will tell you, in his little demure way, " You may not know it, but I gave Poker his name, because he was so stiff." Yes, Paul Adrian and Poker thought that they should go and call on the Doctor and Mrs. McCosh, and they entered the great hall, and before they got into the parlor they met the Doctor, and the Doctor caught them by the hands and gently, but firmly, after his accustomed fashion, led them to the door—not the parlor door—but the outside door, at the same time exclaiming, " What can I do for ye, gentlemen; what can I do for ye? Coom again and see me; coom again and see me!" I suppose he filled up the blank in his own mind with a "when you can't stay so long." After that did Poker's habit a club where dwelt Woodend and Carter and Scharff and Richmond, '83, and other gentry. But soon he departed, and they knew him no more. One day a friend of Poke's did call him Clara out of sport, in allusion to his name, and he took him aside, yes, into his private chamber, and he admonished the friend severely, and did say to him, that if he ever called him by that name again that friendship would cease and the silver cord be broken. So the friend was frightened and promised. But the fellows at Ivy were not so kind, and used to call Poke Lily, in allusion to his Langtry bang, of which it was reported that a Princeton damsel said, " Mr. McIlvaine has a beautiful bang, and it's so becoming. He's the only man in college who knows how to wear one." So Poke grew very wrathy, and he threw fat Billy Riggs under the table in his rage, and he caught little McAlpine by the shoulder with his powerful iron grip, and, with that mighty arm, which, after much contortion, could propel a base-ball at least twenty feet through the air, and he demanded an apology. And the apology was given and the jibes ceased, and they called him Lily no longer or any more. Poker's literary ability was very great. He was as regular as clock-work in taking the *Lit.* prize every alternate time it was offered, and used to go on tremendous sprees on the strength of it with those dissipated men, Wylie, McClumpha and others who shall be nameless. It was said that Poker had a greater command over good English style than any man in College. This I am not disposed to deny, but I cannot but recollect the time when Poker undertook to correct the English of a sentence which Mother Schenck had delivered. One day the time-honored notice appeared on the blackboard in the Chemistry room:

DO NOT CUT AND MAR THE SEATS. IT IS EXPENSIVE.

Poker, who had been busy handing down his immortal name to fame by marking in large letters upon his seat, read this notice, and leaned over to Billy Mac., saying, "Schenck's all off in his English grammar. He ought to have written, '*they* are expensive.'" "No," said Billy, "*it* is expensive," And so Poke found to his cost.

WILLIAM B. McILVAINE, Peoria, Ill.

Billy was head of our Class for four years, and if ever a Class had a fine man to lead it, ours did. We were always noted for having a fine lot of honor men, the necessary exceptions being made, and Billy made a fitting cap to the heap.

H. C. MESEROLE, Brooklyn, N. Y.

Mezzy left our Class twice. Once for three days on account of absences, two of which days he spent traveling to and from home—an event which it bored Mezzy excessively to speak of, *et ergo*, etc. The last time Mezzy left us for good, on account of sickness, and returned afterwards in '86.

JOHN B. MILES, C.E., Peoria, Ill.

"Pat," as we called him, for he was exceedingly *Milesian* in his manners and customs, was a great boy. He wasn't quite so great at first, but he bloomed out wonderfully later, as so many other of our dudes did. Pat became a society idiot in Senior year, and was very popular it was reported, though it was also rumored that the girls used to call him "Mucilage," because he stuck so—came early, I suppose, and staid late, as they do in the Western wilds. Pat became quite a tough, too, at least comparatively speaking, and this, added to his proverbially impecunious condition, often put him in a dilemma. As, for example, he and Rassle Dickey decided to go up to the Yale game together. They bought return tickets, had fifty cents apiece to get into the game with, and fifteen cents besides. They thought this was sufficient, and as man must eat to live, I fear me they had designs upon some free-lunch counter. But where did they pass their time between the end of the game and the starting of the Owl train. Perhaps they walked the streets. Who knows? Ask them.

J. H. MILLER, Springfield, O.

Washee-Washee entered our Class at the end of Junior year, and his leading and engrossing idea was well set forth by the name which was given him.

JOHN KIMBERLY MUMFORD, Syracuse, N. Y.

Mumford entered in Sophomore year, with a rush. Everybody thought he was going to carry everything before him. He gained a band of devoted adherents at once, and Whig Hall thought that his was to be the might which was to vanquish Clio, and bury her out of sight. There was a good deal of ability about our champion; but, alas! he was also very lazy. It was this unfortunate trait which betrayed our Mumford at Commencement, and caused the hopes of Whig Hall to languish. He left at the end of Junior year, and is now reported to be running a skating-rink paper in his native heath.

JAMES P. MURRAY, Princeton, N. J.

Jim was a very convenient man to have around, he always possessed so much information about the manners, customs and doings of the Faculty. "A member of the Faculty told me that we weren't going to have any Bible to-morrow morning;" or

"A member of the Faculty told me that the English examination was going to be a very hard one, so that men shouldn't elect it for a snap;" or "A member of the Faculty told me that it was likely the nine would be allowed to play professionals;" or "A member of the Faculty told me this," or "A member of the Faculty told me that," and so on, no one, of course having any idea who the "member of the Faculty" was. Jim was never very prominent; in fact, he never gained any great distinctions, though his soul longed for them. Yet once he had one in his grasp and hurled it away. At the Class elections, when it came to electing a Washington Birthday Orator, Jim was nominated. Loud was the applause, but Jim declined. Jim was renominated. Howl after howl went up for him. The enthusiasm was so great that even chairs and tables were broken to pound upon the floor. Jim still declined. Again and again did they nominate him, amidst a furore of excitement, but Jim still declined. Finally they gave it up and ran in Shag Wilson, who at first also declined, but afterwards accepted. Jim hied him home and reported that he had had much honor offered him at the hands of the Class, but had declined, whereat a "member of the Faculty" told Jim that he had been very foolish, and had better have accepted the only honor of his course. And Jim, too, having cooled down, agreed with him. So the next day did Jim go privately to Shag and kindly let him know that in case Shag was desirous of resigning, and of being relieved from the onerous duty of speaking, he would be glad to relieve him. "Just resign in my favor, old fel, and it will be all right," Jim said; but Shag didn't see it in that light, so they parted. And Jim remains in private life to this day.

HOWARD G. MEYERS, Albany, N. Y.

Having meditated for a long time as to what I should embody in my history of Myers, and as to what would bore him most, for that is my unhappy office, I have decided to write nothing at all, thus accomplishing the object I last mentioned and adhering strictly to truth. For further particulars, see Thompson, the other Siamese Twin.

M. B. NAHM, Bowling Green, Ky.

Nahen entered our Class in Junior year, took high, and showed himself generally a fellow of a good deal of ability.

PAUL T. NORTON, C.E., Elizabeth, N. J.

Norton was with us but a short time. He stood head of the Scientific School, but left at Christmas, Freshman year, on account of his eyes.

ROBERT M. PARKER, Newark, N. J.

When Bob went into a thing he went into it with a vengeance. When he loafed he loafed hard. When he did other naughty things he did them hard. When he polled he polled hard, and to good purpose. It came into his head to do this last in Senior year. He took the hardest electives, and stood fourteenth in the Class. He had a twin brother at Harvard so exactly like Bob that when he came down here the fellows used to speak to him on the Campus, and he could attend lectures and do various other brotherly offices for Bob. It would be interesting to compare these two and compare the Harvard influence and the Princeton influence on each. Unfortunately opportunity lacks. Birdie got a splendid grind on Bob once, at least he said so. The history of this grind I will not give, but those who know it are rather inclined to think that the grind belongs in the other quarter, I believe.

JOHN M. PENICK, Louisville, Ky.

Penick entered '85 the middle of Sophomore year. He played on the Lacrosse Team at one time, and therefore was classed among that undeservedly despised body the " Lacrosse Fiends!"

THEODORE PERSHING, Pottsville, Pa.

Ted was another of those exasperating men, about whom his friends would tell you that there was lots to say, that it would be easy to write him up, but would never give you any satisfactory information. Ted was of an amative and sentimental nature; this his poems in the *Lit.* testified to, and, also, Jim Cleveland was in the habit of calling him a "regular old Mormon." Ted was quite unwilling to acknowledge this propensity of his, and got quite riled when a prophesy was made about him that, in ten years, he would be married and, with wife and children, would be living among the Blue Mountains. Nevertheless, in a conversation with Chumpy once, he betrayed himself. Chumpy was planning about what he was going to do after he was graduated, and was laying out about seven or eight years of study for himself. Ted had been agreeing, with a pleased smile, to all these plans, but at this point he grew grave. Scratching his head he said, with pathetic earnestness, "Great Gad! McClumpha! a man's got to marry sometime; what are you going to do about that?" Ah! Ted, you gave yourself away that time, old man. Ted's beard was a source of great delight to himself and to his friends. It made him look so old and wise. In fact, a Freshman once took Pop for a Professor, from his aged appearance, and Ted was reported to have got through College on the strength of the learned air that beard gave him, " waiving by its aid the formality of an examination."

JAMES POTTER, Baltimore, Md.

Here I shall have to quote again from that article in the *World*, to which I have made such frequent allusions, and which dealt much with several defunct (as far as the College is concerned) members of our Class. It slandered James, perhaps, but then I don't think he minded that sort of slandering very much. "Perhaps the bloodiest man in College now, all things considered, is James Potter, of Baltimore. He will graduate in '85. He has large wealth in store for him when he reaches the voting age, which will be in a little over a year, but for the present he has to worry along on an allowance of $5,000 a year. He doesn't take much to horse-flesh, but is fond of sport; fonder still of having a good time with the boys, &c., *ad infinitum*." Jim got into a row with his namesake the middle of Junior year and left us. The following is from the Philadelphia *Press*, of June 3d, 1885: "Mr. James Potter, of Baltimore, formerly of Princeton, '85, was married yesterday evening, by the Rev. Joseph May, at the First Unitarian Church, Philadelphia, to Miss Lily Sturgis, daughter of Mrs. Robert S. Sturgis. Several college men attended the wedding and reception. The ushers were Messrs. Charles and Robert Sturgis, Mr. N. Brooke Dolan and Mr. Louis Baker, of Philadelphia, and Mr. Frank Duane and Mr. J. Borden Harriman, of New York."

CLARENCE PRICE, Cincinnati, Ohio.

Pricey used to be called '84 Price because he ran with Buck Blackwell's crowd so much. But he got over that after a time and was universally regretted when he left us at the end of Sophomore year.

WILLIAM P. RIGGS, Baltimore, Md.

Billy might be said to be the oldest-looking man in our Class, he was so full of wrinkles. And he was old in guile, also, though young in age. Billy was fond of going off and having a quiet little time by himself, and he told no one in advance and seldom afterwards. If he were with any one and that one betrayed him, Wrinkle had no more use for that man. Out upon him! Wrinkle's adventure down the Kingston road one evening, where he was chased for a mile by an angry father, and lost nearly fifty pounds of fat, is very interesting. You should get him to relate it to you. A foul slander was perpetrated against Wrinkle by the *World* newspaper once, which, in its obnoxious article, declared that he aspired to be a social leader, and spent freely with that end in view. The absolute falsity of this charge will, of course, be patent to all.

WILLIAM H. ROBINSON, West Hebron, N. Y.

Robinson entered our Class in Senior year, and proved a good speaker and writer. He receivd the third Baird Prize.

ADDISON F. ROBERTS, New York City.

Josey was walking in the Campus one day in the first week of Freshman year, when a Sophomore who passed him with a friend stopped and said, "Allow me to introduce to you my friend, Miss Josey Bangs," alluding to the most prominent feature about Josey at that time. The name was so appropriate that it clung. People forgot what Josey's real name was, and Green, the carpenter, who, as usual, wanted his "little bill," was heard inquiring where he could find Mr. Bangs' room. Quite a convenient scheme, wasn't it? Josey departed at the end of Sophomore year and has just returned, pretty thoroughly disgusted, from a ranching experience in the Wide West, where his father sent him to keep him out of harm's way.

FORD W. ROCHELLE, Sparta, N. J.

Ford's history was intimately connected with that of the bookstore at 3 N. E. Like a true Spartan, he bore the opprobrium that was cast upon him for the high prices he charged. But at last, spurred to desperation, he issued a defence. It was anonymous, but surely his. It was about the "Little Tin Gods" who got into difficulty with the "exchangers of the laws and principles of the thunder and the lightning and the much unknown for gold, aye, gold;" and how, in the end, the exchangers got into the "Little Tin Gods." It did not persuade the fellows that Ford was not a Shylock, rolling in wealth, but it was a mightily well written piece. Where Ford's wealth came from 'tis hard to see, for he never was able to collect more than half his bills; but such was the general opinion, and let it pass.

J. C. ROOSA, Monticello, N. Y.

* * * * * * * * * * * *

PAUL A. SCHARFF, Newark, N. J.

Paul Adrian was of the purest and noblest, *i. e.* the muddiest, of Dutch blood. In fact, with commoner mortals he did not associate much. He gave Poke McIlvaine his name, and ho took Wilder home with him once for a visit. Thereby hangs a tale which shall be told later. The tale is known to me, because Paul Adrian was in the habit of telling his most intimate affairs to every one. Affairs which this history shall not record, first, because they were known to all before; and second, because they might not suit, and I might get shipped for them, like the *Princetonian* editors; and third, because they might hurt the feelings of such a thin-skinned fellow as our friend Paul Adrian.

F. W. SCOTT, Richmond, Va.

When Scotty and Mezzy walked together upon the Campus, as they were fond of doing in Freshman year, there might you see a contrast. For Scotty was one of those men who had to stand twice to cast a shadow; who was liable at any time to be arrested as a tramp for going around without any visible means of support, and who very likely got his clothes at half price as being such a big ad. for the tailor. And that is all I remember of Scotty. He left at the end of Freshman year.

ALEXANDER SCHENCK, Princeton, N. J.

Schenck was not in our Class for very long. He entered College, so the report was, to play base-ball, and, on the strength of his brother's reputation, he got on our Freshman nine. He did not make a success in that line, however, and went away towards the end of Freshman year.

HOWARD SCRIBNER, Yonkers, N. Y.

You never could tell when Scrib was here and when he wasn't. He was like a Jack in the Box, always appearing when you least expected him. Scrib would go away for a month, then come back and loaf around for a couple of weeks, and then blow off again. He blew away finally for good, and is swelling it in New York, by latest accounts from Frosty.

JOSEPH B. SHEA, Pittsburg, Pa.

Jo kept a sort of "Rest" up in his room in West. Not an "Angel's Rest," but a sort of home for the lunatics, for those who had lost their brains, having had them stolen by something they put into their mouths. These used to gravitate insensibly towards Jo's room, for he was such a good-natured, happy-go-lucky individual that he hadn't the heart to turn them out, but had a sort of fellow feeling for them in their distress. What if he were to come to the same fate! It would be hard to believe, but it might be so. Jo always had a great number of stories to relate, which he commenced on with the most serious and important air in the world, but which hardly ever led to anything. Thus, after the summer vacation in Junior year, he returned to College and told us jubilantly that *he* didn't intend to study this year, he'd fixed the Faculty all right. They wouldn't dare to drop him. When asked the reason of this belief, he replied, with the utmost earnestness, that he had seen a respected member of that body taking a glass of beer in a restaurant during the past summer. "Oh, I've got him by the ears!" cried Jo. But his trust was mistaken. He received, I think, two unpleasant notes at Christmas. And yet, though Jo has several times threatened to expose that member of the Faculty in the papers, for revenge, he has never yet seen fit to do so. Jo was a very lazy person, as maybe gathered from what has gone before. He was not particularly fond of his studies, and, like the poet Gray, his idea of heaven was to lie all day on a sofa and read novels. Jo, also, liked to sleep late in the mornings, he did not like to get up early, and often wished he had a deaf ear like Billy Taylor, '83, who, whenever he missed Chapel, used to send in as excuse that he had been sleeping on his good ear and couldn't hear the bell. This peculiarity of Jo's was manifest after the Glee Club concert at Louisville. He went to bed so early there, and got up so late, that it was a joke with the Glee Club to allude to Jo's "Long Sleep." How early was it you went to bed Jo? Morning or evening?

ALFRED B. SHERWOOD, Scotchtown, N. Y.

Sherwood entered the beginning of Sophomore year. What there is to say of him is little, but it is naught but good.

AUGUSTINE C. SMITH, New York City.

One of the most amusing incidents connected with Gussie's career occurred while he was a member of '84. It is of such an interesting nature, however, that, with the leave of '84's historian, I quote: "A practical joke played upon Gussie caused him temporarily much anguish of soul. It seems that Gussie had done something naughty in examination. Consequently, conscious of his sin and moral degradation, upon receiving his mail at the post-office, to find a letter from Prof. Packard stating how, after great hesitation, the Faculty were convinced of the truth of certain evidence presented to them, for they had believed Mr. Smith incapable of doing wrong. But justice must be vindicated, and, after all, it would be better for him to pay the penalty of his sins. They were, therefore, obliged to suspend him for a month. Gussie was informed that he must leave on the early train on the morrow, and immediately repair to his parents, who had been already informed of the affair. Gussie's anguish on receiving this epistle was extreme. After supper he repaired to the billiard-room, where one after another the fellows went up to him, expressed their sympathy and retired. The ovation, for it was nothing else, lasted for an hour. Pleasant as were the condolences of his classmates, Gussie realized the stern fact that on an early train he must depart. Accordingly he tore himself from the embrace of his friends, and retired to his room, where the sorrowful operation of packing his trunk must be accomplished. Thoughts of home and returning to it under a cloud, above all anticipations of parental displeasure, filled Gussie's thoroughly unhappy mind. When, lo! a knock on the portal. 'Come in,' a sad, plaintive voice from within uttered. The visitors were Dave Look and Alec. Ernst. They glanced at Gussie's countenance, which, flushed during the ovation, was pale and haggard now. They glanced also at the preparations. They had not the heart to remain silent. They told Gussie that he had not done such a wicked thing after all. They told him that Prof. Packard had not written the letter. They did not state, however, who did. Gussie was now completely mystified. When, however, they said that he was not shipped, Gussie's joy was almost delirious. Could it be! Still a Sophomore! Still a member of Princeton! Slowly the joyous reality penetrated his dazed comprehension. He was not angry at the perpetrators of the joke. He blessed them for it, for his sorrow was now transformed into joy. Of all who lay down that night to sleep Gussie was the happiest, the most thankful, the most serene." Apparently Gus soon forgot the terrible feelings which had been raised in his breast by this cruel hoax. Do unto others not as ye would they should do, but as they did unto you, was his motto. Verily, Gus was a schemer, and a hard-hearted youth. He delighted to see others suffer, but took good care that they should not know that he was the cause thereof, for he was wily. But the vanity of his partner in crime caused his betrayal. It seems that in Senior year, about two weeks after the Ethics examination, the brilliant idea occurred to Gus and Arthur Tree, those men of mighty intellect, that it would be a keen scheme to frighten some unwary youths who less excelled in that particular, and distribute a few gratuitous conditions in Patton's name, merely to save him the trouble, of course. So they devoted a day and a night, as much time as it had taken them to poll the examination which they deemed so hard, and they concocted several little notes, which ran probably as follows:

> Egoistic utilitarianism strictly obeyed would induce you to be at my house on Monday night, when you will hear of something to your disadvantage.
> F. L. PATTON.

Lord, Urquhart, Gooch, Foltz, Kempshall, and several others, received these communications. They kept very quiet, but it was remembered afterward that they had not received their mail on Saturday morning with any loud demonstrations of delight. Now it really showed great intellect and keenness in Arthur and Gus to have gotten this grind up in such good shape. Really one wouldn't have thought it of them. But Gus even went further. The joke had created such consternation that Gus began to fear the consequences. He began to fear lest, if it were found out, the stalwart Buzzy might meet him on some dark night, and, being wrathy, give him his deserts. So on the day when they were all to go down to Patton's, Gus went too, and every one thought that he, the biter, had been bit, and suspicion fell not upon him. But vanity overcame his coadjutor, and he told the historian and requested him to put it in the History, as such a capital joke (so unlike the stories which the coadjutor was famed for telling). So the historian complied, and leaves you to judge for yourselves.

BENJAMIN B. SMITH, Louisville, Ky.

Ben loved athletics next after talking much and loud, and making a great deal of noise about all he did. To hear Ben talk, you would think he had never been beaten—that he was unsurpassed. For in cases where the nominal victory went to another, the judges, of course, were at fault; the great Benjamin could never be mistaken. In base-ball, Ben's record was not fine. His fielding was very weak, and his batting not particularly strong; but whenever you twitted Ben on this point, he always had an answer ready. It seems that in the long, long past ages, when he was at school at Freehold, he made a base-hit, and this base-hit came up on all occasions, and was always present to Ben's memory. Ben had a fine arm, of which he was not a little proud. So proud, in fact, that when he went to the sea-shore he used to spend all his time on the beach in a sleeveless bathing suit, and turn hand-balances on stools, to show his muscle to admiring crowds.

CHARLES H. SMITH, Philadelphia, Pa.

Charley was one of our prominent athletes, or would-be athletes. He was elected a base-ball director at our first class-meeting, but resigned soon after, and privately informed the historian that it wasn't etiquette for a man to be on the team who was also a director. Poor Charley! he went out and practiced faithfully, but he resigned to no purpose. He might as well have remained a director, for etiquette would not have interfered. Even after that disappointment, Charley would say that he might have been on the nine, but was unwilling to play any position but first base, though they begged and implored him to take right field. He was careful, however, not to make any of the above statements when Van Etten, the captain, was about, at which time they might have been contradicted. Charley was fond of making excursions in the direction of the village of Hightstown, whenever a ball was about to take place there. Not that he could dance much, his "good corporation," as the General says, forbade, but because he deemed it a good and gracious thing to lend his countenance to scenes of rustic merriment—and refreshment. On one of these occasions he was accompanied by our friend Jack Blye. Having countenanced the rustic merriment—and refreshment, till quite late, or rather early in the morning, they started collegewards. There was no moon, in fact it was very dark, but Jack and Charley put confidence in their steed, and decided to rest their weary, weary brains with a little slumber, and to let the beast plod quietly on by himself. Their confidence was ill-reposed. When that vicious racer heard gentle snores behind him and felt the reins relax, then fire came from his nostrils and his eyes flashed, and a plan of fiendish malice entered his brain. An owl gave a loud tu-whit tù-whoo from a tree hard by, and the racer stretched out his neck and yawned, and he lay down in the road and slumbered with much content and a feeling of satisfied revenge, for he knew that they who had driven and beaten him desired to make chapel the next morning. And when they awoke the sun was shining, and they saw what had been done and that they were still where they had been, and they thought of the notices of twenty absences that were to come, and they sighed grievously. Charley departed in Junior year. He came into a fortune afterward, it was said, and went to visit his brother-in-law, in his castle on the Rhine, where he is having a glorious time *suo genere* with the Gretchens of the Rhein wine.

EVERETT L. SMITH, New York City.

Smithy's was essentially the "Pursuit of Knowledge under Difficulties," if anybody's pursuit ever were so. A College education is a grand thing, a College diploma is much to be desired, and the air one breathes under the classic shades of a College town is very salutory no doubt. Smithy certainly believed in these three propositions, and put his belief into practice. Eight years he spent in Princeton, in Preparatory School and College, and one summer in Princeton, Mass. In fact, we would have thought that the very word Princeton would have come to be looked upon with disgust and loathing by our youthful friend. But it was not so. Bravely he stuck by the ship, and soon will he have weathered the point, have secured the sheepskin and be afloat on the broad ocean. At one time, indeed, it did look as if Smithy's bark would never round the headland, but a skillful pilot was secured, a pilot of great size and mighty brain, and he took the wheel for a time, and put Smithy on the right course; and when he went away all was well, even better, perhaps, for Smithy, as was natural, occasionally liked to "paddle his own canoe."

ROBERT L. SMITH, Appleton, Wis.

Of Smithy be it said that when the Professors would reach his name they breathed a sigh of relief. He was the last of that mighty company of Smiths, some of whom were handed down to us from '84, others of whom were bone of our bone and flesh of our flesh. Fifth Smith was Bob. But there was even another, G. Smith, whose form was never seen by mortal eyes, but who once was with us in the spirit, as shall be told later.

FRANK H. SPEER, B.S., Pittsburg, Pa.

Speer used to talk a good deal, and say a good deal more than he meant. He would whip around from one opinion to the direct opposite in the space of about ten seconds, and he always had some quick, witty reason ready for what he did. He affected a manner of speech and conversation which, to say the least, was abrupt, and, for the above causes, was probably considered as amusing a fellow as there was in the Class. He had a good deal of ability, when he chose to exert himself, and in argument he alone could bear away the palm from Ben. Smith, the clarion-voiced.

CHARLES R. SPENCE, Baltimore, Md.

"Bunny, Our Darling Wab.," like John Dickey, was exceedingly afraid of the historian. He knew the historian was in possession of much information in respect to him, and could give him away "cold," as the saying is, if he chose, and Bunny was not particularly desirous of being so disposed of. On the other hand, however, Bunny was a good deal bigger and fiercer than Dick, when his ire was roused, and the historian was slightly in awe of him. Besides, Bunny propitiated the powers that be by lending them his scrap-book, out of which the historian culled much valuable information. In this scrap-book, if you read between the lines, you could trace Bunny's career. First in order, and preponderating in number over the other cuttings, came certificates of good conduct, examination papers, reports from the Registrar, with grades of 99 frequently to be seen. Then, towards the end of Freshman year, athletic items, principally relating to lacrosse, usurped the top place. This state of things continued throughout the book till, in Junior year, invitations, cards, reception bids, dinner bids, etc., etc., outdid all the rest in number. Poller, Athlete, Society Idiot, was Bunny's course, and it was noticed that a change took place in Bunny after he reached this third stage. He grew a little deaf, and was in the habit of saying "What? what?" on slight provocation. He adopted a cunning and melodious drawl in his speech—corruption of the melifluous Baltimorean. He fell in love for a while, but soon fell out again under the tender care and exhortations of the fellows at the club, who, of course, were careful to spare his feelings and never tease him on the subject. His eyesight also grew rather bad. It was even said that one morning in Philadelphia he donated a quarter to a street urchin to black a pair of patent leather shoes. Fact which can be explained on no other basis than that of excessive weakness in the occular nerve.

A. L. STAVELY, Lahaska, Pa.

Ask Buck about the time the report went around that the daring, bold and prominent Freshman, Stavely, was to be hazed by the Sophomores on a certain night, and remind him of his abject terror on that occasion, and how he went over and slept with that stalwart hammer-thrower, Charley Leeper, for protection. Ask and remind him I say, and observe the result. If Buck gets angry, fierce and wrathy, then what will he do with me, who published it? I fear to say more of him. I had better let him rest in peace.

EDWARD C. STEERS, New Orleans, La.

De mortuis nil nisi bonum.

WILLIAM DE W. STERRY, New York City.

Truly in Freshman year Bowery was magnificent. 'Twas then that his glory chiefest shone. Athletics and general toughness did he most delight in. On the day when we were to elect base-ball directors Bowery appeared in knickerbockers and a sleeveless undershirt, showing his mighty arms, and making a deep impression on our unsophisticated minds. We all gathered on the grass in front of Granny Hunt's room, and watched Bowery taking in, or not taking in, the balls which were knocked him, and getting them over to first with that great underhand twist of his that was never equalled. "Sterry," thought many, "had a tight grip on short-stop at the very least," but so it did not prove. Then Bowery played foot-ball, still with that sleeveless undershirt, until it was torn from his back, and he purchased a canvas jacket instead. Bowery was very like the ostrich, on the foot-ball field. He would put down his head when he received the ball, and make one plunge forward, usually landing in the protecting arms of a player of the opposite side. Athletics were not Bowery's forte in Freshman year, despite his passion for them, but in Junior year, as captain of Stonaker Club nine, which defeated Ivy and Van Dyne's, after exciting contests, he came out strong. His exhortations to Stub and Griff to " Play ball; Play close; Run it out; Come in on a hit," delivered with the appropriate bowery accent and gesticulations, from which he derived his name, were worthy of the New York League at least. Bowery played no mean game at short that day, and, when the foe crept nearer and nearer, his courage supported the failing spirit of his men. Pat Miles made his famous catch in left field. Stub made a grand one-hand stop at second. Jim Buckelew chased a base-hit over a barb-wire fence, tearing his fat carcass sadly on the way, and Stonaker's won. Bowery ran with our friend, Chas. Smith, a great deal in Freshman year. As the result of this intimacy a rather amusing incident came under the notice of the historian. Neither of the above-mentioned gentlemen were behindhand in their capacity to consume the noxious weed done up in paper, and known to the initiated as "cigarettes." Now, their own abundance often failed to supply them, so that they were obliged to call on their friends for aid in this direction. In fact, at that period of their existence they were each in eminent danger of becoming that most horrible of all pests, a sponge. One day, as the historian was seated on a chair in the University billiard-room, peacefully watching a game of pool, our fat friend, Charles, approached him, and, in a melodramatic whisper, said, "You're Class Historian, are you not? Well, I've got an immense grind on Sterry; I'll tell you if you want me to." On the historian's signifying his eagerness, Charles proceeded. " Well, he's a regular sponge. And, if you want to grind him, just call him 'Have-you-a-cigarette Sterry' on Class Day." And he glided away, and the historian meditated on Charley's kindness in so speaking. And then of a sudden did our athletic friend, Bowery, approach, and, in a melodramatic whisper, said, "You're Class Historian, are you not? Well, I've got an immense grind on Charley Smith; I'll tell you if you want me to." On the historian's again signifying his eagerness, Bowery proceeded. "Well, he's a regular sponge. And, if you want to grind him, just call him 'Have-you-a-cigarette Charley' on Class Day." And he glided away, and the historian meditated on the profound truth that "Birds of a feather flock together."

JONATHAN STURGES, New York City.

As this gentleman's intimate friend, the Censor, will undoubtedly bring up before you, on Class Day, all his history—past, present and future, all the crimes he has committed, and the sins he has done—I deem it better to leave him to his fate, not attempting to defend him by portraying his eminent virtues and spotless character against the assault of slander and malice. Nothing more, I can assure you.

GEORGE E. SWARTZ, Danville, Pa.

All honor to thee, Swartz, thou fair maiden! For, like Portia, didst thou save us from the clutches of Shylock, who desired of us our pound of flesh. In other words, thou keptest the opposition book-store. Swartz was of a very grave and sedate nature. He condemned all noise and disorder. Whenever the man who sat next him in class made any demonstration, Swartz would say to him, in a very nasal twang, "Don't *dew* that. That's fresh." But occasionally, it is rumored, Swartz was known to unbend from his strictness—nay, even from his dignity—and to come down on a level with common mortals, in company with his cronies, Rochelle and Wilbur (Rochelle, of course, before the rival book-store difficulty put an end to their friendship). It occurred one night to these mighty men that it would be good fun to sack King Blades' room in Edwards Hall. Needless to state that King was out and that they had no intention of letting him know who did it, for they feared his arm. So they went into King's room, and they removed the bedding and the sheets, and they took down the pictures from the wall, and they piled these, in company with all the chairs and crockery that was in the room, in the middle of the floor, and *everything* liquid that they could find they poured over the heap, and they wet the matches, and went away and waited results. Now, shortly afterward King came back. After much trouble he got a light and saw the state in which the chamber was. Also, he had a shrewd suspicion who were the perpetrators of the deed. So he mounted to their rooms, and by the power of his terrible eye he compelled Rochelle and Swartz to come down, but Wilbur by main force. And when they had entered the room, King was pleasant, and they all joked right merrily about the trick. So, when their fears were lulled King slipped out, and he locked them in. And though they banged much upon the door, and though Swartz, even the maiden Swartz, used words which he should not, King had no mercy—he was deaf to their cries, and they staid in the cold, wet room, without a light, until the morning.

HENRY D. THOMPSON, Catskill, N. Y.

Thompson always had a great deal to say about how everything in College should be run, foot-ball, base-ball and the College papers included, but as for subscriptions, out upon them! he had no use for them. Probably we would have won every championship there was to be had, if only the authorities had taken things in hand and listened to Thompson's suggestions. At last, however, Thompson took charge of Lavake's foot-ball team, and conducted them to victory against Van Dynes' without a single mishap. Yes, there was one—one slip in the plan of action, one step was not carried out. Thompson was playing opposite to virtuous Jim Bayard, in the rush line, and undertook to bull-doze him. Unfortunately, Jim did not see it in that light, and offered some mild resistance. This astonished Thompson, and he proceeded to use physical means to carry out his plan. But Jim again astonished him by using the strong arm on his side, for Thompson had relied on Jim's forbearance, and in the end Jim overcame Thompson, and cowed him so that he said no more and did little the rest of the day, as those present can testify.

HENRY HERBERT THORP, New York City.

Thorpey was a crank, indeed. In fact, he always went by that name among his friends. His passion was shooting, though in Freshman year Tom Berry divided his affections with his gun. Thorpey acted like a lover towards his "darling boy," so much so that the fellows got to calling Tom Miss Berry; but the fit soon died away, and Thorpey went back to his dog and gun. Thorpey had an unfortunate little dog, whom he used to call, indifferently, Vere and Monk—possibly the last because he allowed the purp to have no communication with other dogs, always making him come up and sit beside him, on a separate chair, whenever he entered a room. Thorpey was, after all, very successful with dogs. Indeed, he kept Tree's dog Dick within decent bounds for one whole day, a task no one else would have ever attempted. But with the gun one could tell a different story of Thorpey. He used to wander off with Kittle into the country, spend whole days there in fact, and bring in absolutely nothing, though he used to promise us most delicious game for supper whenever he set out. Kittle reported once that Thorpey had had six shots with a revolver he carried at a rabbit at ten yards distance, and with no avail—a story which Thorpey was wont to deny with many blushes. Thorpey made a bad break once—a break he couldn't deny very well, a break which brought him before the eyes of the world in the pages of the *Princetonian*. Ask Thorpey, the great naturalist, about the time he called an owl which Kittle had shot a "broad-faced partridge," and note the terrible anger which will arise and the sneer upon Thorpey's innocent countenance and his muttered darn fool, for even to such a length would the mention of the above fact cause Thorpey to go. Harry left us at the end of Sophomore year, and is now studying medicine in New York.

L. H. TOWLER, Corunna, Mich.

Towler blew in among us from the West in the middle of Soph. year. "From the West," you said, as soon as you looked at him. "Aye from the very far West," for Towler laid no restraint upon his conversation and manners. He'd been "traveling for a firm" I'd have you to know, and knew the ways of the world. And "they did say he made a capital salesman," as Washee Washee, who knew him, informed me. Well, I should have thought he *would* make a good drummer. That white hat and long coat and business-like air all pointed that way, and besides, as Washee Washee said with a triumphant air, " He never lets go of a feller when once he gets a hold of him ; I tell you, Towler's a sticker." Sometimes Towler would wax generous, in which case he would usually say, " Come on up street. Like as not I'd treat ye." But usually he confined himself to strict business principles. He left us in the middle of Senior year, having received an advantageous offer to " travel for a firm."

HENRY P. TOLER, C.E., Madison, N. J.

Harry was one of our men whom we unwillingly, very unwillingly, resigned our grip on at the end of Soph. year. He was hurt in the pole vault at the intercollegiate games, and was obliged to go away for a time, and then came back in '86. He took the clapper in Fresh. year, and was on the foot-ball team in Soph. year. But the most prominent part of his history has been since he was connected with '86.

HOWARD P. TRASK, Fulton, Ill.

"Cupid," called not for his beauty but for his being of a very short sight, must have shot his darts in solitude, for the historian never heard or saw them, and so must leave Cupid's history unwritten. He went away in Junior year.

ARTHUR M. TREE, Chicago, Ill.

It is with fear and inward trepidation that I approach to write the history of the immaculate Arthur, dude and masher of '85. Unequalled after Potter left. Yes, Arthur kept up the credit of '85 with the fair sex, for he was a true squire of dames. He needed them. They kept him from feeling lonely all alone here in the East. Nay, also, he encouraged any little familiarities they might long to shower on him, not standing on his dignity, but accepting all with kindly good will. One afternoon at Commencement in Fresh. year, Arthur, who at that time was quite a chum of Coyle's, '84, was engaged in earnest conversation with a damsel who had been under Coyle's protection, and whom it was rumored Coyle loved with the depth of his whole heart. Coyle watched them, and he feared that all he desired was slipping away from him, and he stole nearer and listened, and he heard these words uttered with an accent and with an expression which could belong only to his rival, "Ah, don't call me Mr. Tree; call me Arthur, your own Arthur." Then Coyle clenched his teeth and stole nearer still, and he heard, "Fondle me, Miss Mary, for my relatives are not here." Then anger suffused Coyle's noble, handsome feature, and he pounced on the unwitting Arthur in his wrath, and the damsel also pounced on Arthur in her wrath, for she liked not that style of conversation. And it nearly came to a duel; but that was happily avoided, for blood might have been shed and '85 might have lost her Arthur. But Arthur did not confine himself to mashing alone. In the Fresh. year much else did he do, and he was, with several other unfortunates, in the greasing-the-track episode, and what they did there shall be told later.

THOMAS C. UMSTED, Smyrna, Del.

Umsted's full name was Thomas Chalmers, and he was called Pete. He certainly did not resemble the eminent divine in disposition or manners, and there was no reason why he should have been called Pete, except that perhaps he absorbed the name from Pete Bergen, as he did much else that was valuable. For Pete was of a gay and lightsome disposition, "popular and convivial," as the *World* puts it, and needed many shekels, and had them not always. Pete left us at the end of Sophomore year, and is now in business in Philadelphia, where he sees much of Charley Smith, lately returned from the Rhine, and is the same old boy, they say. There is one reminiscence connected with Pete which it would be too bad to leave out, though two others, one a Shade, were concerned in it. One day when the second division of Sophomores went into French they found to their delight and surprise that Hermann Huss, instead of Kargé, had the chair. Pandemonium, of course, reigned at once. Matches were let off, apple cores were thrown, cat-calls and whistles made the air ring. An alarm clock was let off and all the fellows called out "Dynamite! Dynamite!" in excited tones. Hermann grew very nervous, but he stuck it out. He had been through this before in Fresh. year. Finally, after all else failed, Petey rushed to the window, threw up the sash, and pretended to be violently sick, making a great racket, coughing and spitting like a cat. The Class, in the meantime, getting a fine view of Petey's noble form, were in shrieks of laughter, and Hermann sat in his rostrum, stuttering and sputtering with rage. Finally Petey pulled in his head and, wiping his eyes, with a most dolorous expression on his visage, called out to Hermann, " I've just had a hemorrhage of the lungs, Professor," and took his seat. Hermann stuttered out, " Vat vas your name—your name? I gifs you a zero, and I send you away, and I gifs you tree disorder marks, and you needn't nefer come back! Vat vas your name!" And then, as Petey hesitated, Hermann shrieked to him, "I summons you, chentlemen, tell me his name. Vat vas your name, you scoundrel?" Just then a lucky idea occurred to Petey. " G. Smith," he replied. " Ferry vel, G. Smith," said Hermann, " you go at once." And Petey went, glad to have shifted the blame upon the mythical G. Smith, whose name was on the roll, but who had never appeared at College. But, alas! his joy was not for long. Bob Parker, in the first division, at the next hour, likewise got into trouble with Hermann, and, since great minds think alike, and since he had not heard of the foregoing incident, he decided to use the same dodge, and visit his trouble upon the innocent Shade of G. Smith. So Hermann condemned him. But when Hermann came to look over his paper he found that G. Smith was endowed with about twenty disorder marks and eight zeros all in one day. This seemed, even to the German mind, impossible, so he investigated and he found the truth of the matter, and those two youths were about to be punished; for, as Hermann said, " You hang by one string in dis college. I tell you I cut dot string." But they apologized and all was well·

GEORGE URQUHART, Wilkesbarre, Pa.

Urquhart entered '85 in Junior year, from Yale. He got on the *Princetonian* in Senior year, and handled the exchange department, when his reviews of the *Yale Record* and *News* were of such a truculent and blood-thirsty nature as to give warrant for the suspicion that he had tried for a position on the above papers, and got left.

CHARLES VAN AUSDAL, Dayton, Ohio.

Charley was one of the Dayton boys, Preach Hawes, Sam Smith, the two Bicks and the rest. Charley never went back on the good old gang, and when they got playing horseup in North-West, I tell you they made the fur fly. Tutor Fine lived in terror of his life, and quiet boys, like Knapp and Bayard, on the top floor, would barricade their doors. Charley used to do various other things with the good old Dayton crowd, and great was his sorrow when they went away. Charley's moustache was the pride and joy of his heart, the very apple of the eye, by whose aid he used to contemplate it for a half an hour at a time, standing before the looking-glass in his room. Yes, Charley was a handsome youth, and withal a genial companion; and what if it were rumored that he was well aware of the former fact? It makes not against him. Does any of us think himself actually ugly? I have no grinds or stories to tell about Charley. Steady and staid was his course throughout. A moral youth always, of course, till he became corrupted into a member of the base-ball nine of '84; I need say no more, that is stab enough.

JOHN G. VAN ETTEN, B.S., Kingston, N. Y.

John left us, much regretted, at the end of Sophomore year. He was on the Glee Club, and was a good base-ball and foot-ball player. Had he remained here, he would have been one of our crack men. His was a loss to '85.

WALTER S. VAUGHN, Richmond, Ind.

Vaughn remained here about a month. He was then taken with a severe attack of homesickness [he was a little fellow] and went away for ever.

L. RODMAN WANAMAKER, Philadelphia, Pa.

The fellows always and justly thought that Rod. was unfairly treated by the Faculty in being obliged to leave our Class and enter '86. He skipped the examinations at Easter and June, in Soph. year, on account of severe trouble with his eyes, and, though afterwards the Faculty allowed '86 men who had done exactly the same thing to rejoin their Class, they refused him permission, and he had to accept the bitter pill of going back a year, not graduating with his Class, and, incurring the suspicion away of having been dropped. I am glad to have an opportunity here of giving my testimony in regard to the facts in the case, for we never lost a finer man.

PAUL WEIR, Owensboro, Ky.

Pee Wee, when first seen by Princeton eyes, was a short, fat, broad-faced youth who wore a light suit, an extremely flat pancake hat, and who used to float about the corridors of the University Hotel, talking much in notes whose liquid softness proclaimed that he hailed from the land of the Sunny South. And Pee Wee drew the attention of the Sophomores upon him by his artless ways, and was the first to suffer. One evening he received a visit from John Harlan, Kid Cauldwell and other noble spirits of '84, whose zeal finally ended in their mistication. Pee Wee was a little too keen for even the immortal John· Without waiting to be asked, he at once volunteered to perform all the necessary ceremonies, such as singing, reading Greek, "setting up," drawing a few chaste sketches, etc., and carried out the programme after an order of his own. When the Sophomores had got quite disgusted with Paul's taking of matters into his own hands after this fashion, and with such exasperating complaisance, they resolved to go away. "Halt!" cried Paul, as they reached the door, "ye forget I am a Christian youth; something yet remains to be done." And he got out of bed, where they had safely deposited him, and requested them to light the gas, whereupon he slowly and carefully perused the ninety-five verses of the 119th Psalm, and offered up devotions of a half hour's duration, while the Sophs., whose conscience had smitten them, and who actually believed that Paul was a boy of extremely pious habits, stood devouring their impatience at the door. If one were to look in '84's Class History one would see that their historian does not dwell on this incident with any great degree of pride, for Paul, as the saying is, rather "got into" those men of '84.

JAMES M. WICKER, Sanford, N. C.

Wicker, also, was from the Sunny South. He came among us in the middle of Fresh. year, and he was a marvel to many of us, for he was not like all others from the Sunny South, for, lo and behold, he was not "one of the boys," as they were, and it seemed a strange thing.

CALVIN WIGHT, New Hamburg, N. Y.

* * * * * * * * * * * *

WILLIAM L. WILBUR, Hightstown, N. J.

"We are sorry to cast discredit upon such a worthy institution as Princeton College, but at present two of its students stand accused of robbing the P. R. R. station at Jamesburg. To make a long story short, these young men stole from the station a sign bearing on its face this laconic but terribly tyrannical law, "No Smoking Allowed." The thrilling narrative of their escape by train, and their detection by Conductor Riddle at Monmouth Junction will, no doubt, be told differently in College halls, but as given by Station-master Voorhees it would make some young men in Princeton College feel shaky. Perhaps the young men may be forgiven if they apologize." Such was the terrible tale unfolded in the pages of the *Jamesburg Record*, which Wilbur took special pains to forward to the historian that it might be inserted in the History. For Wilbur was the hero of the above escapade, and he loved to see himself in print, for the longing of his heart was after prominence. Did he not organize a Freshman Glee Club, and tax the members twenty-five cents apiece to get their names in the *Bric-à-Brac*, carefully inserting his own among the number? though he afterwards met a like fate with Hiram Gooch, and was requested to resign. Indeed, Wilbur's voice was not of a very melodious character, and it is said that when he was hypnotized by Holmes, and endeavored, under his influence, to sing the Flower Song in Faust, in imitation of Madame Patti, that the effect was simply paralyzing, excruciating, binding to the last degree, as Wilbur warbled serenely away among the high notes, kissing his hand to the audience in the approved fashion, and ending at last in a shriek of agony that brought every man in the entry banging on the door. Wilbur was of an *elastic* nature, however, like that school of philosophers he told Jimmy about, and defeats had no power to crush him; even the evil result of his superhuman struggles for the Class-Day Committee left him still alive. He bobbed up serenely. Within a week that brow, on which sat the ghosts of many votes, cleared, and Bombey was himself again.

ROBERT P. WILDER, Princeton, N. J.

Wilder was a good boy; a boy of whom none would have suspected aught that was amiss. True, his actions on the day of the Class cut might have been open to misconstruction, but then that is nothing. But, alas! one day, in conversation with our friend Paul Adrian, did a terrible fact come to light. Paul Adrian waxed very confidential, as was his wont, and told us in his little demure way a tale which runs as follows: " I took Wilder home to make a visit with me once. And we had a very nice time. And we used to mow the lawn and weed the garden, and hear stories in the evenings about the old Dutch blood, and it was such fun. But Wilder did not weed the garden very well, and I never knew that he loved exercise, or that he was very strong. And one day I wanted to go and pick blackberries in the woods, and there were some girls at the house, and they said they would go, too, all but Lucy; and Wilder said he would stay, too, and keep Lucy's company. So we went, and I came back early, for I was very, very tired; and I came round through the garden, and there was an arbor there; and as I was going by I heard a sort of a noise like when you want a horse to go faster, a sort of a smack; and I went into the arbor, and Wilder was there, and he was *wrestling* with Lucy!" Paul Adrian concluded, with an air of great surprise and wonderment, poor innocent soul. Ah! Wilder, Wilder! When thou goest out among the dusky tribes of India, to convert them, beware that thou hast naught to do with "wrestling," which is a euphonious term for "the spirits rushing together at the touching of the lips," else mayst thou find the keen blade of some angry brother penetrating thy most Christian ribs.

EDMUND WILSON, Shrewsbury, N. J.

"Is it fair? Is it just? Is it right?" Ed., to use the words oft used by thee in those telling speeches, those speeches which often gained as many as seven votes to thy side, is it fair, I say, that I should deal hardly with thee? With thee who lovest grinds on others, while of thy own dignity thou art very chary. Do I not know that thou wilt be well taken care of by our mutual friend the Censor, who possesses a tongue nearly equal to thine, and an unsparing hand. Peruse the Censor's speech, kind reader, if thou wouldst know of Ed., the mighty man of such intellect that he could pull the string and cause Jackson and Shag Wilson to jump when he pleased, who wished to make the *Princetonian* a power to be felt, and who succeeded, for it was felt—by the Faculty.

FREDERICK H. WILSON, Philadelphia, Pa.

Poor Shag's occupation in Senior year consisted in driving a team of horses, some of whom were too spirited and too much for Shag, others of whom were so lazy that all the whipping could not make them work. There was all the time, likewise, a power behind the throne who advised Shag and caused him to turn his team this way and that, and it was rather amusing to hear Shag say, in his meditative, self-contained way, hissing out his sibilant "Yes, I decided to let that go in," when you knew all the time that the power behind the throne, who had produced the above "that," would have had something of an extremely forcible nature to say if "that" hadn't gone in. From this it may be gathered that Shag had no mean estimate of his own powers. He produced a poem for the Baird Prize. Now, his delivery of this poem was not of a particularly felicitous nature, as those who heard it well remember. After the decision was given out, Shag was heard to remark, "Yes, I didn't know that the judges would make such a great point of the writing. If I had, I wouldn't have made such a point of delivery." In the great, unequalled, illustrated number of the *Princetonian* appeared, under a cut whose drawing was fearfully and wonderfully made, the following joke: "What are you reading, old man?" "Carlyle's autobiography. It's immense." "Is it? Who wrote it?" This break was attributed to a Freshman, and was thought rather good. So it was; and would that my conscience as historian would allow me to keep secret the fact I am about to disclose. In conversation with Ted Pershing, a year or so ago, Shag happened to notice that Ted held a book in his hand. "What's that?" said Shag. "Trollope's autobiography," replied Ted. "Is it? Who wrote it?" asked Shag. Ted replied naught; he thought a good deal, however, when he saw that joke appear in the *Princetonian*. Shag! Shag! an '85 man, too! Unconscious mental cerebration must have been at work when you evolved that joke, Shag.

EDWARD S. WOOD, Trenton, N. J.

Billy was quiet—too quiet, in fact, for the good of the historian, who labored and strove over him, and was forced to let him go by. They used to call Billy "Mick" for a long time after he was seen on a high stool in the offices with his arm round Jimmy's waist. What doing, I know not.

WILLIAM E. WOODEND, Huntington, L. I.

Phenix he was called, for he must have been very young when he entered our Class. The youthful prodigy of '85. Juvenile in looks, but old in guile, for it was not because of his learning, but because of his skill at poker, that he was a prodigy. How Woodend did delight in running the Freshmen of '86, when they entered. He was so very fresh himself, that the similitude was strange, and the contrast not marked. Though he used to threaten to murder the historian if he reported any "lies" of him in the History, truth remains and must be told, that Woodend used to rope those tender shoots, fresh from home, and to retire to neighboring cities, and spend the fruits in high living, gaining thereby the name of Phenix, the bird who lives alone on the face of the earth, and has not his like. But this wickedness came later, for at first, Phenix used to get roped himself, for he was innocent, and the story of one of his ropings runs as follows: how one day Phenix desired to become acquainted with a fair maiden, who lived in the direction of the Seminary, and Chapin said unto Phenix that he would secure an introduction for him, for Chapin said that he knew the maiden, and that her name was Mary. So, one day Chapie told Phenix that he had seen Mary, and that she was desirous of meeting Phenix, and that Phenix should go down and whistle outside the house that night, and that Mary would appear, and Phenix did, and stood and whistled for two hours, but nothing came, not even a wind. Then was Phenix wroth. But Chapie told him that there was some mistake, and that he should go and wait the next night, outside the Seminary hedge. And Chapin took Horner, '86, who was of small stature, and dressed him in a complete set of women's clothes (and where Chapie got the clothes the deponent saith not), and told him of the plan. So Horner came out at the appointed time, and Chapie introduced her to Phenix, and Horner afterwards said that when Phenix took his hand, he trembled exceedingly, and, after a few minutes' converse, Chapie said he would go away, but Phenix desired him not, in a trembling voice, and Chapie waited a little longer, and then insisted on going, so he walked away, and, when he had reached the triangle, he heard the steps as of one pursued, behind him, and Phenix ran by, fiery with haste— he had caught on. I grieve to say he had attempted to embrace Mary, and had felt the muscle of Horner's arm, and perceived the stubble of his beard. Never before had Phenix been crushed; never before could you shut his mouth, but now, Phenix was no longer himself. Mention the word Mary and he blushed a fiery red, and was silent from his much talking. In the words of the poet Nelly Bedle, in the *Princetonian:*

> "Mary had a little lamb,
>   His fleece was white as snow,
>   And every where that Mary went,
>   The Lamb he Woodend go."

FRANK S. WOODRUFF, Elizabeth, N. J.

Frank roomed with Beattie, and therefore, need I mention it, was a lady's man. He blushed so furiously when you bid him beware of much dalliance with the dusky maidens in Asia Minor, where he is going to teach, that he must have felt there was some likelihood of his susceptible heart being led astray. Nay, but Frank was no Lothario, I would have it understood. His was no hard heart, who led away poor maidens into the paths of love and then deserted them himself unaffected. He was the soft-hearted one, not they; and the damsels knew this and feared not Pop. Did not I hear of a society of fair dames who met together weekly, and were making Nice Warm Quilts for the Heathen in South Africa? and was not Pop the only male admitted to this society to aid in the Making of Nice Warm Quilts for the Heathen in South Africa? Because, to use the words of the Presidentress, "he was quite harmless."

CHARLES R. WYLIE, Pottstown, Pa.

I have alluded several times in the course of this History to that class of men on whom it is almost impossible to find grinds. Wylie was certainly one of these. Yet certain characteristics of his lead one irresistibly to conclude that he must have made breaks at times. For Doc. was not one of those quiet, self-contained men who never become prominent, and who bottle up every feeling and wish in their breasts. Nor was he meek and gentle, if he were wise as the serpent. He knew what he wanted, and voiced it pretty effectually. He liked to manage, and, indeed, might be classed with Jackson and McAlpine, to form our trinity of managers. Perhaps a certain pomposity and self-sufficiency is the invariable concomitant of the managerial ability. At any rate Doc., like our other two friends, possessed it to a great degree. "I'm running this thing, I'd have you to know," he used to say, and that was sufficient. Now it follows from this that in Doc.'s long experience his angles must have rubbed here and there. If so, however, we never heard of it. Wylie did dearly love a grind on somebody else. How he would rub it in, and run it down to the ground, through all its intricacies. But he himself was as wiley as the serpent, and laid low. He exposed himself to attack on but few points, but on these, ye gods! how touchy he was. Doc. came home frcm the Yale game in Senior year, and told several good stories on Jingle Harris. Now Jingle, hearing of this, became wrathy, and decided to give the true history of the case. He told how Doc. became very lonely at New Haven, and constantly besought him, in pathetic accents, "Now don't you leave me, Jingle. They have designs on us, Jingle." And he told how to curb Doc.'s wit by calling him "Velveteens," probably in allusion to the lining which Doc. wore on that day. Doc. was very fond of music, so much so that in Freshman year he was very chummy with Rochelle, who used to play the fiddle sweetly to his edification, down in Edwards Hall. After this, however, Doc. became struck on his own voice, and remained content with the ethereal sounds he himself gave forth in the solitude of his chamber. How well, in the summer season, when the windows were open, did the unfortunate denizens of East Witherspoon become acquainted with the "Midshipmite," and the amount of money (one penny, I think,) which it took to convey one to Twickenham town. Besides his voice, Doc. was also famed for his ugliness. In this connection a terrible stab was perpetrated on Wilbur, our handsome youth, by one of the Faculty, who said that he really had great difficulty in distinguishing Mr. Wylie and Mr. Wilbur, and that he couldn't quite make them out yet. On this hint all the fellows called Doc. "Wilbur" thereafter, not as a grind on Doc., of course, but merely to bore Wilbur a little, you know.

FREDERICK A. YOUNG, Princeton.

As '84 lost their Smiths, so we took no firm hold upon our Youngs. Fred. left us after a short sojourn. He is now in '86.

GEORGE D. YOUNG, New York City.

George did not remain with us to graduate. He left in the middle of Junior year. His history up to that time is not eventful; had he remained with us longer I might have more to say.

INCIDENTS.

ON THE Friday night after College opened, in September, 1881, '85 decided to have their Fresh fire. Mat was conveniently sick. It was even rumored that some daring youth from our number had doctored him that he might be unable to attend. This being the case, everything went merry as a marriage bell. Around the cannon was placed an enormous heap of dry goods boxes, gates, fence-rails and other débris collected from all quarters of Princeton. Fire was applied. The whole Campus was soon ablaze with light while we, under the guidance of Ed. Peace and Lorry Riggs, marched round and round it two by two, many of us without coats, shoes and hats, and called loudly upon the cowards of '84 to come out and view the scene. Suddenly a dark cloud in the direction of Reunion was observed to grow thicker and blacker. It began to move. Then every '85 man knew that it was '84, and, though he trembled, he girt up his limbs for the contest. Round and round the Campus each class marched. Neither being, apparently, very anxious to begin. Suddenly, when '85 was in front of East, the lights were put out. Our Class was formed under cover of the friendly darkness in a solid phalanx, and we advanced to meet the foe. We approached at double quick, breaking into a run as we drew nearer. We struck them full on, and here the spirit of '84 men was shown. Their front men, finding ours too much for them, commenced to use their canes. We poor Freshmen, ignorant of our rights, stood the blows in silence till Ed. Peace, Jim Flint, Lorry Riggs and a few other Juniors of that stamp jumped in and so effectually demolished the '84 leaders that canes were put a stop to.

The two classes separated; after another ten minutes they met again. This time '85 completely walked away with '84. They marched straight through them like an avalanche, hurling them right and left, and driving the remnant who still hung together against a huge elm tree. For the third time we met them, while the fire was burning low and only faint gleams lit up the Campus. This was the most intense struggle of all. Loud was the noise and din of the conflict. Great was the heat. Fat Billy Riggs, who was in our front rank, was heard to exclaim, "Let me out, it's too warm in here; I give in." Long was the battle, and at the end there was no decision, for, while '84 rushed us into the corner of Old North by the pump, we rushed them out against the trees. Be that as it may, we had taken away their prestige, we had rushed the Sophomores once. The record was broken.

Not long after this the Campus of an evening began to be lively with Juniors preparing and training Freshmen for the cane-sprees, which were to take place on the evenings of October 8th and 9th. In consequence of this an amusing incident took place behind Whig Hall. Gill and George Howell had a couple of Freshmen in hand, and had pitted one against the other for mutual advantage. They themselves bent over them in loving attitudes, and whispered words of comfort into their ears while they fought. Now, it happened that our venerable President was out walking and enjoying the air of a fine autumn evening, and, hearing the noise of a scuffle, he peered through the darkness, and discovered what he took to be three Sophomores engaged in murdering or otherwise maltreating one of "me Freshmen." He approached quietly, but with anger in his breast. He caught hold of Gill by the collar, and endeavored to drag him off, at the same time exclaiming, "I know ye. What's your name? I know ye. I'll have the whole Sophomore class sent away from me Collij. Come away now, sir." Now, Gill was much astonished at this sudden onslaught, and, thinking for the moment that it was Howell playing some practical joke upon him, he called out, "What the deuce are you doing, George. Leave my Freshman alone, will you?" And, so saying, he flung the supposed George, who was Jimmy, twenty feet away down the bank. Oh, horror! when out rang the accents of that clarion tongue, "I know ye. Come away now, sir." The four youths did not *come* away, but they *went* away about as quickly as legs could carry them. And they disappeared into the darkness, and Jimmy wended his sorrowful way homewards.

On October 8th, the Preliminary Cane Spree was held. After a gallant fight, under the moon and the "sliding stars," Toler lost his cane to MacMillan. Then Frank Miller appeared on the field. At this time Birdie was not the man he afterwards developed into, but had he not been rattled would have undoubtedly taken the cane from Miller, who was not noted for his excessive strength. As it was, Birdie lost his cane after a stubborn contest. Things looked blue for '85. Perhaps they were to have not a single cane to show. But, no; Jack Blye redeemed the honor of our Class. He took the cane from Parmly with the greatest amount of ease, and was carried to his room on the shoulders of his admiring classmates. To give a detailed account of every fight in the general spree of the next night would be impossible. The fights, however, were won and lost as follows:

1. MacMillan *vs.* Toler, won by MacMillan.
2. Finney *vs.* Jackson, won by Finney.
3. Prentiss *vs.* Granbery, cane was cut.
4. Smith *vs.* Young, won by Smith.
5. Nichols *vs.* McFerran, won by McFerran.
6. Thomas *vs.* Spence, won by Thomas.
7. Kennedy *vs.* Cleveland, cane was cut.
8. Monger *vs.* F. Wilson, cane was cut.
9. Hutchinson *vs.* Smith, won by Smith.
10. McKay *vs.* Hughes, won by McKay.
11. Baldwin *vs.* Knox, won by Knox.
12. Dunn *vs.* Carter, won by Carter.
13. Egbert *vs.* Murray, won by Egbert.
14. Blackwell *vs.* Halsey, won by Blackwell.
15. Lundy *vs.* Bissel, cane was cut.
16. Marshal *vs.* Van Ausdal, won by Marshal.
17. Tod *vs.* Blades, won by Tod.
18. Gulick *vs.* Ellet, won by Ellet.
19. Van Kirk *vs.* Dawson, won by Van Kirk.

'84, twelve canes; '85, seven canes.

Our Class nine was soon afterwards picked, as follows: Potter, H.; Toler, C.; Edwards, A.; Griffith, B.; Van Etten, P.; Schenk, S.; Cooper, R.; Clark, L.; B. Smith, M. The game with '83 was very close. The game with '82 was a walk-over for the Seniors. The game with the Sophomores was close and exciting till towards the close; '84 finally won by 7–2.

Later on it became time for the Freshmen to take a cane into Chapel, and so fill the cup with the achievments of '85. Ben. Smith, formerly of '84, was the man found brave enough to do this deed. In fact, I am not sure but he himself concocted it. October 22d was the great day; afternoon Chapel the fated hour. Ben. came in with the cane tightly clasped under his coat, the end, however, projecting, and he hastened down the aisle and took his seat. The Sophomores had at once caught on. Word was passed to the two upper Classes, who occupied seats near the door, to remain in their seats when prayers should be over, that the aisles might be clear. Duff. was in the pulpit, but his words were not heard. While the benediction was being pronounced, both Classes stood on tip-toe. When the amen was said, both rushed with a yell to the doors, they crushed through and outside. Ben. Smith and Jim Harlan were at one end of the cane, Mac Millan and Bryan at the other. The rest, not being able to get their hands on the cane, engaged in a free fight outside. The result could not long be doubtful. '85 was gradually securing the cane and the victory, when Mat. appeared and carried off the trophy. Meanwhile Jimmy, armed with an umbrella, had been floating round the outside of the jam, prodding the insurgents in the legs and ordering them to go to their rooms. "Come away now," he said, "I know ye, at least I know within one or two o' ye. I'll expel ye from me Collij. Go to your rooms and wait there till I come," etc. All which exhortations had, of course, not the slightest effect. When, however, Mat. carried off the cane, the excitement subsided, and we Freshmen withdrew to a class-meeting in the English Room, when, among other business, your unworthy historian was elected to the place of honor he now fills. Meanwhile the Sophomores, a howling mob, were outside, endeavoring to get in, but Clarence Price, with Billy Riggs on his right hand, and Charley Smith on the other, did keep the door. Clarence even went so far as to go outside and shove MacMillan down the steps for impertinent curiosity. Meanwhile it grew darker and darker, and finally we broke up. As we came out the Sophomores were ready for us. Each man with his cane knocked off a Freshman's hat, and then, while he stooped to pick it up, the Sophomore started howling for the cannon at the top of his speed. Thorpey was the only one who left his hat to the tender mercies of the wind, and he, oh glorious youth, reached the cannon first. We all piled after him in a body, and then commenced, in the gray of that October twilight, the great Cannon Fight. Each Class strove to have the last man on the Cannon. Long was the struggle. Great was the prowess shown, and mighty deeds were done. About ten Freshmen and ten Sophomores had hands on the cannon. The rest were endeavoring to remove them or enable them to retain their hold. The fight waxed very fierce. Blows were frequent. Bucky Bradley, a Fresh. Soph., besought Rod. Wanamaker, whom he took for a Sophomore, to aid him in removing Miller, a man in his own Class, whom he had mistaken for a Freshman. Rod., seeing his mistake, was, of course, glad to assist him, when, suddenly, Bucky was admonished as a fool by Miller and turned on Rod., who calmly took him by the scruff of the neck and deposited him twenty feet away. The fight ended with Thorpey's hands still on the cannon, though his clothes were scattered to the four winds. As a result of the above pleasant incidents, Ben. Smith was summoned before the Council in the Star Chamber, *i. e.*, the Faculty Room, and, to his great delight, was excluded from the privileges of College for a fortnight.

Not long after this our foot-ball team, consisting of McAlpine, Bird, Van Etten, Wanamaker, Clerihew, Lawton, Toler, Baker, Clark and Harriman, opened the season with a victory over Pennington to the tune of 6 goals 7 touch-downs to nothing. We defeated the U. of P. Freshmen 3 goals to 1 goal, and the Lawrenceville 3 goals 2 touch-downs to 1 goal.

From this time on through the rest of the course, '85 was always prominent in athletics. We got a man on the University nine in the spring of Freshman year (a great triumph for Freshmen), and in the same season defeated Lawrenceville in a ten-inning game by a score of 5 to 4. In the fall of Soph. year we had a strong class foot-ball team, besides three men, Bird, Toler and Baker, on the Varsity. The same year we defeated '86 at base-ball by 17 to 5. We took the largest number of prizes at the winter sports the same year, and had as a member the champion amateur pole vaulter, H. P. Toler. At the beginning of Junior year we were much crippled by losing many good men. The result was that we did not get as many men on the team as we had expected. Still we recovered from this loss. We took the Peace Cup in Junior year, and under our management in Senior year, Princeton retrieved her defeats of the previous season. Bird led the foot-ball team to victory. Harvard and many other smaller colleges were easily beaten.

On Thanksgiving Day, '85's team, consisting of DeCamp, Wanamaker, Harris, Adams, Bird, Irwine, Hodge, rushers; R. Hodge, quarter-back; Toler (taking Baker's place, who was hurt), Lamar, half-backs; Moffat, back; met Yale on the Polo Grounds, at New York. Every one remembers and will remember that great game. Every one remembers DeCamp's touchdown and Moffat's goal from the field, which every person on the field, Yale men included, except the referee, considered undoubted. Princeton outplayed Yale at every point. The game was called on account of darkness, with twenty minutes yet to play. The score then, according to the referee, was 6 to 4, in Yale's favor. He declared it "no game." The Yale men, while accepting the score which he gave, inconsistently refused to accept his decision of "no game," and claimed the championship. Princeton challenged them to play the game to a close, but they refused, knowing too well what the result would be; and, in the eyes of every impartial person, Princeton was the champion of '84.

In base-ball results were not quite so gratifying. Captain Edwards had to make a team out of almost nothing. Bickham, the phenomenon, was discovered, and to Edwards is due the excellent batting and base-running of the nine. The smaller colleges were easily defeated. Harvard vanquished us badly in both games, but everything was forgiven the nine when they wiped the ground with Yale on June 6th, 1885, to the tune of 11 to 5, making a total of 20 hits off Odell, the crack pitcher of the New Haven men. The nine, in this game, played as follows: Shaw, H.; Bickham, P.; Toler, A.; Edwards, B.; Taylor, C.; Cooper, S.; Clark, L.; Reynolds, M.; Van Ausdal, R.

From athletics and rows with the Sophomores, I now pass on to chronicle some of the great achievements which the immortal Class of '85 accomplished about town, prefacing my remarks, however, by stating that the clapper was taken in all due form, and with appropriate ceremonies, in the month of October, by Harry Toler and Steve Halsey. '83 were bound that we should do all that Freshmen ought in this line, they marshalling us and getting the fun, we being the cat's-paw, and getting shipped. It occurred to them one night that it would be a fine thing to set us ringing the fire bell down by Ivy Hall. So, under the leadership of Lorry Riggs, a crowd went down to perpetrate the deed. Potter, Toler, Gibson, Tree, Thorp and Riggs were there. Thorpey was set to climb the trellis and attach the wire. Just as he had tied the wire to the clapper, and, clinging with all his might to the trellis, was preparing to slide down, a man stuck his head out of the engine-house and called, "I see you there." Thorpey laid down flat on his stomach, and the others, in fear and trembling, hid themselves in ditches and behind hedges. Apparently the man's suspicions were lulled by the complete silence, and he retired to bed. "Stay up there," cried Lorry to Thorpey, "while we pull." At the very first peal the wire broke and those on the ground fled for their lives, leaving poor Thorpey to slide down unaided and run after in mortal terror lest he be caught. Thorp was wont to say after that experience that he had enough of those men. "They are no gentlemen," he would affirm with great earnestness, though soon afterwards he forgot his wrath.

Many other things did our Class do of the same stamp as the above. They were resolved to keep up the honor of the old flag, and they did so and gained an unenviable reputation about town. But the crowning act of all was the great greasing-the-track episode. This idea originated in the fertile brain of Arthur Tree, who, in company with his fellow-conspirators, Bill, Healy, Scribner and Frost, met together on the Thursday night after Thanksgiving in Frost's room in the hotel. They had purchased ten pounds of lard and ten pounds of soap grease. They heated it in silence and mystery before Frost's fire, and stirred the mixture with his poker. They carried it out in a pail down the track to the curve and they laid it on thick with a brush for about two hundred yards. Then they retired to a haystack in a field near by and sat in the pouring rain waiting developments. The light of the train was seen slowly leaving the junction; it moved faster and faster. It crossed the bridge and commenced the ascent. Suddenly the wheels slipped. Back went the train to the foot of the hill. The engineer threw down sand and started again. Just as they reached the same point back went the train again. Then did the engineer curse right roundly, and so loudly that those in the haystack heard him with fiendish glee. But he tried it again; no use. Then the passengers, a thin man and a fat woman with a green umbrella, got out of the train and started to walk. Suddenly they disappeared. Oh, horror! where were they? Then were the sounds of oaths, mingled with shrieks, heard issuing from the ground, and the train men rescued them from the culvert into which they had both fallen. Then did our conspirators leave the haystack and go to the hotel and watch the movements of that unfortunate train; and when they went to bed it was still there. But by morning the grease was scraped off and the train reached the station, only three hundred yards away, at about eleven o'clock—thirteen hours late. But vengeance fell on those conspirators, not through a detective, as we all thought for a time, but through Mat, and they went to their homes for a while. Many other things were done, such as tying the whistle of the engine open so that it blew all night, to the great annoyance of all around, and such which it boots not to record. And as a climax and end to it all came the horn spree.

On the night before Marquand's Latin examination in Fresh year, about 11 o'clock, forty or fifty Freshmen were assembled at Connover's field, well equipped with horns and blacked faces and slouch hats. From here they marched quietly down Bayard avenue to Billy Sloan's house. They entered the grounds and marched round and round the house, calling for a speech, and blowing loudly upon their horns. Then they gave three cheers, and went into Baby Rockwood's, where the performance was repeated. Here, I regret to state, one or two members of the Class who were not exactly *compos mentis* broke a couple of lamps. This set the rest going, and every lamp in their line of march met a like fate. From Baby's they marched up

Stockton street a little way, and then back and through a little alley behind the hardware store to Canal street. Here they visited Cam., whose plate-glass window they effectually disposed of. Next came Granny Hunt's turn, and then they marched down Railroad avenue, being reviewed as they passed Mrs. Smith's by Tubby Anderson, who sat in the window, but was afraid to come out, as he was already in difficulty with the powers that be. From here they went up on the Campus as far as West College, when something scared them, and they all ran. Only to meet again, however, in front of the hotel on Railroad avenue. They gave Duff and Dad a send off, and then some wished to disband, but others called them cowards, and these prevailed, so they started up Nassau street, where they were met by Cooper and Robeson, '83, who were out gunning after Brackett's Physics paper. Now did Cooper see his chance. He resolved to use the Freshmen as cat's-paws, himself being the monkey, which he very much resembled in appearance. He instilled into the minds of the Freshmen leaders that they were to go down to Brackett's and raise a terrible row. While this was going on, and under cover of it, he and Robey intended to break the windows of Brackett's study. Then, in case Brackett did not come down and shut the shutters, after the Freshmen had gone away, they intended to get in and filch the paper. In this scheme it is reported that they succeeded. Meanwhile '85 proceeded to Jimmy's, treated him as they had the rest, and, just as on their way homeward, they reached Murray Hall, Locherby and Captain Coffin turned the light of a dark lantern full upon them. At once there was a stampede. John Dickey and George Young ran so fast that they fell down and the rest over them. Indeed that is probably the reason of the small stature which they retain to this day. Baker alone was actually caught, and this resulted in the betrayal of the following men, all of whom pleaded *non vult* at the Trenton court the next month: Lamberton, Potter, Toler, Fisher, Buckelew, Sterry, J. Foster, Halsey, Dolan, Gledhill, Granbery' Gaither, Blye, Hall, Dawson, Burleigh, Dickey and Roberts. A fine of $200 was imposed upon these unfortunate youths, a fair share of which was born by those who were not caught, and, in addition, they were all requested by the Faculty to leave these classic shades, and seek the seclusion of their homes for a month.

Soon after this it entered the fertile brains of several of our class that it would be a fine thing to have a Burial. No sooner said than done. Euclid and Lysias were the books decided on. Orators were appointed, among them Griffith, who was the poet. The poem which he composed ran rhythmically, as follows:

> There are two books which Freshmen study,
> With these two we are done,
> And one of these is Fine's Euclid,
> The other ἔλαβον.
>
> To-night we're met to bury these,
> With hearts by no means sore;
> For everyone among us knows
> That they have been a bore.
>
> Now, let us sing and all be glad,
> And in the fire them throw;
> For who among us will be sad
> To part with λαμβανω?

It was decided that we were to meet at 11 o'clock on the Varsity grounds, equipped with torches and arrayed in night-shirts and masques. Jim Potter, as Grand Marshal, was to lead the procession, on a horse, to Stockton's field, where the speeches were to be made, the poem to be read, and the infant Euclid, in the shape of a rag baby, was to be cremated. A programme in the shape of a coffin was engraved. Everything was prepared. Then the leaders, having in mind the fate of the Horn Spree youths, decided to ask permission of the authorities. And the authorities, having in mind what our Class had done, and might be expected to do again, refused permission, and the '85 Burial died unborn. From this time onward the history of of our class as a class became uneventful.

The following documents tell it as well as I can. For, in Sophomore year, our absorbing interest was the repression of the Freshmen—well expressed by our Proc.; and in Junior year appeared that wretched anonymous letter, the authors of which were probably '85 men. The rise and fall of this document, the absolute breaking down of all the charges made therein, and the shame felt by the college at large for what they had done, are voiced in the last set of resolutions passed by the mass-meeting in Mercer Hall:

I.

RILED! RATTLED! RUSHED!

PREAMBLE.

When, in the course of human events, it becomes necessary for the unsophisticated to be dissolved from the apron-bands which have hitherto bound them, and to assume before their masters the ignominious and servile position to which the laws of the College entitle them, a decent respect for the opinions of their superiors is demanded and required. We hold these truths self-evident: That all men are created equal, save FRESHmen; that these are endowed with certain unmistakable characteristics, among which are:

GALL, GAWKINESS, GULLIBILITY.

BORED! BEARDLESS BOYS! BIZ! BOOM! BAH!

(Ad)VANCE you Strong Porter, and (T)RUNDLE in the BALLANTINE beer; take a S(T)ARTER, you LAUGH(L)ING (M)APES from FARR-AND near, and celebrate your GREEN(NESS). For, if you find your MATH-IS hard, Oh, SHAW! (G)RANNY HUNT is easy.

At the SYMPOSIUM, (SAMMY'S text,) to be held around the Cannon on the occasion of the FRESH Fire, the following distinguished KIDS will be toasted(?):

WORDROW, the sole representative of the (twice) six thousand.
ADAMS (Jumbo), who wept on leaving the Queen's garden.
LARKIN, the greatest FEET-ure.
JESSUP, who stands twice to cast a shadow.
HOODOO, who has succumbed to the charms of Delilah.

MEADE, one of a job lot from Persia.
CONGER, a man who "smiles and smiles, and is a villian still."
MORGAN, not "Jonny."
HALSTEAD, who drinks nothing but *Champagne Cocktails*.
YOUNG-ALLEN, "the Discard."

MAC will officiate as GENERAL mixer and tosser of drinks, into the spittoon.

N. B.—FIRE to be lighted at 4 A. M. Trouble begins on MAT'S arrival. Date uncertain, but mercury at HUDNUT'S indicates a cold day.

PROCLAMATION.

In view of the utter helplessness of the timid FRESHMEN, they will be permitted to carry canes, provided they are lame, or umbrellas, to be used as such, if the weather is cloudy, on and after 18—.

II.

" During the present academic year more men have been dismissed than in eight previous years, and the College has lost in tuition alone thirty-two hundred dollars."

There are immutable laws which govern the phenomena of nature. The volcano, with the awful and potent causes which underlie it, is bound to erupt even through incalculable obstacles. Human nature, that has its grievances, is like to this volcano, and must carry to the outer world some token, at least, of the fires that burn within. But the outbursts of human nature are, as the present instance indicates, subject in some measure to the will, and yield to emotions which distinguish the human mind. The students of Princeton have long enough confined their feelings to conceal disrespect, quiet sneers, and subdued profanity toward that body whose position should call for personal respect.

The *Princetonian* when, in a way forcible, but just, tried to voice the grievances of the students, was threatened with dissolution and its editors with disgrace. A nameless man took once a method covert, but honorable, of publishing to the world the corruption of the English polity. We take the same method of publishing to the Faculty of Princeton College the wrongs of their students. Concealment is fitting. Punishment, in keeping with the general tenor of college government would, without doubt, follow hard upon the writers of this letter. The College is in a crisis. By their recent action the Faculty have drawn upon themselves the censure of every fair-minded student. The occasion demands the publicity of these views; we publish them.

We condemn the methods of examination adopted at the close of the fall term. They were severe, injudicious, and not calculated to obtain the best results. This was especially noticeable in the two upper classes, where many of the best men broke down, and were obliged to leave before the close of the term.

There has arisen with this new *regime* a spy system, which is but a tiny reflection of the police service of Napoleon.

A large corps of servants, in the employ of the College, are required to keep a close scrutiny on the students who come under their observations, and to report to headquarters. Rooms are unlocked, desks are opened, and even private correspondence is not inviolate. The presence or absence of playing cards is carefully noted. Inquisitive tutors are seen listening at key-holes. The night watchman is observed on a ladder peeping into lighted windows on the ground floor. Railroad officials are invited to note down all students leaving town, and report their names. Barbers are threatened with social ostracism for refusing to become informers. Self-paid instructors study suspicious windows through opera-glasses. The tradespeople are pumped, and diminutive hotel clerks become willing witnesses. A prize-fighting detective is constantly in the pay of the College. Every class has one, perhaps more, spies whose delicate consciences compels them to tell all they hear. Thus there has gradually grown up a scheme of espionage which, in the malignant mendacity of its prosecution, though not in the greatness of its purpose, rivals the worst days of the inquisition.

We denounce this as cowardly, contemptible and degrading. It indicates on the part of the governing body narrowness of conception, weakness of execution, and a blind ignorance or a willful disregard of the welfare of the students committed to its charge. It generates in the mind of the governed a hypocritical cringing to methods which, in their hearts, they believe to be unjust, and it compromises those manly principles which the lessons learned in a college course are calculated to inculcate.

Ignorance is a poor guide. Age cannot sympathize with the sports of youth, and men whose lives have been passed in the cloistered seclusion of their studies cannot intelligently dictate terms on the subject of athletics, about which they display such profound ignorance. We fail to see how the Faculty have recognized the dignity of our sole instructor in gymnastics; they have not even given him that voice on the subject of athletics which his modest manly worth has long since won for him. And we feel assured that if his opinion had been heeded, a much more intelligent result would have been reached. A thing worth doing at all is worth doing well. A professional is one who does a certain thing so well that he commands a price for his services. Thus we have professional actors, professional ministers, aye, and professional professors. Any one desiring a thorough knowledge of the classics and of mathematics comes to College, where professional teachers are hired.

Is it not just as fitting that those who wish to cultivate their muscles by rowing or playing ball, should study under a man who has made these exercises a specialty? Provided only that this man is of good moral character, and that the oarsman or ball-player does not fall behind in his class. The bright and glistening Mecca, toward which every loyal student looks with joyful anticipation, is the Yale game. We hold that it is desirable to play this game on the Polo Grounds, not, however, "to put men in the hands of speculators," nor to cultivate a passion for excitement, but because a great many alumni and friends live in and about New York, who would be unable to see the game if it were played elsewhere.

True, the gate-money is an important feature. The expense of equipping a team is considerable, and thus the burden which would otherwise be thrown on the students is borne by those who are willing to pay admission to see the rival teams play. It must be remembered that both foot-ball and base-ball are self-supporting only through the gate receipts collected yearly at New York.

With the petulence of a school-boy, "who won't play if you won't play his way," these Solons have resolved that "students in colleges in which these resolutions are in force shall not be allowed to engage in games or contests with the students of colleges in which they are not in force." So we are deprived of our most formidable and therefore most desirable rivals. Thus competition, without which there can be no excellence, is taken from us, and we are condemned to a monotonous routine of games with Lawrenceville and Pennington. It must be remembered that in the vicinity of Boston and Providence will be found ample opportunities to evade the strict letter of these resolutions. Why should Princeton take the initiative in this step? Why should she truckle to Harvard when Yale refuses to follow? Is it wise to thus rudely overthrow the customs sanctioned by long years? How many men will be lost to our College! From the great preparatory schools whence our strength is to be darwn, we can expect no aid if this College ceases to be a rival with Yale and Harvard. What influence will be lost to the College! These are weighty questions. Mark them well, conscript Fathers. How often we have sat around our hearth-fire and listened to our fathers and elder brothers tell of the prowess of this or that champion, and how we have longed to come to College, where those scenes portrayed in Tom Brown and Hammersmith, would become to us stirring realities of which we would be a part! How we gloried in that little piece of orange-and-black ribbon, which we wore so prominently as we sauntered up Broadway, and how pleasant after the game to sit and talk over the day's play! What aspirations were born, what resolutions were formed under the healthy influence of a well-fought game! Do away with all this, gentlemen, and you destroy one of the best influences of a college student's life. Athletics are the escape-pipes for that surplus energy which is bubbling over in the disposition of every true boy.

As among nations, that country reaches the highest eminence which approaches most closely to self-government, so among colleges the highest education is attained when between professor and student there exist feelings of trust, confidence and sympathy; when the student standing on the edge of manhood, is permitted to exercise in his own development those powers of judgment which the law and common sense allow him. These principles the new Dean has utterly violated. Actuated by that

"Vaulting ambition which may o'erleap itself,"

he has pursued a line of action which, if persisted in, will reduce Princeton College in its government to a level with the preparatory school and in its numbers to a scant hundred. And we may well believe that numberless students, realizing this fact, daily offer up the earnest invocation, "Deliver us from our Dean."

With feelings of the sincerest respect for the great and good men who constitute the body of the Faculty, with a still unswerving loyalty to the College of our adoption, we have, in a frank, straightforward way, presented these our grievances. The citizen who has been a college boy, himself; the professor, whose kindly feelings are not warped up by a desire to excel his colleagues, will understand us; the alumnus, proud of his *Alma Mater*, and desirous to see her retain a position of independence among the great colleges of the country; the honest father confident of his son's honor; the thoughtful, manly student, will appreciate and approve the motives from which this letter was born. That is sufficient.

III.

We the students of Princeton College, in mass-meeting assembled, endorse the following preamble and resolutions, to be presented to the Board of Trustees:

WHEREAS, Facts have been brought to our notice implicating members of the Faculty and employés of the College in a system of espionage which we deem cowardly, contemptible and degrading, viz.:

1. That servants are employed to keep a close scrutiny on the students who come under their observation and to report them to headquarters.
2. That rooms are secretly unlocked and desks are opened by force.
3. That playing-cards are secretly taken from rooms.
4. That officers of the College have been seen listening at doors and have gained admission to rooms under false pretexts.
5. That the night-watchman has been seen standing on a ladder, peering into lighted windows on the first floor.
6. That railroad officials have been invited to note down and report to headquarters the names of students leaving town.
7. That a barber has been requested by members of the Faculty to give information against students, and has been threatened for withholding such information.
8. That at a previous session of this mass-meeting a student publicly declared that a professor had offered to secure for him, free of charge, a furnished room in a college building, provided said student would report to him personally any irregularities which he might observe in that neighborhood.
9. And that letters have been sent by a member of the Faculty to former members of the College, offering a premium for information against their friends in College.

WHEREAS, We feel humiliated and degraded by this system of espionage; therefore,

Resolved, That we hereby petition your honorable body to institute a thorough investigation of these charges, with a view to removing the above alleged abuses; and

WHEREAS, We disapprove of the adoption of the new Athletic Regulations;

Resolved, That we petition that they be rescinded.

G

IV.

PRINCETON, N. J., March 4th, 1884.

WHEREAS, after thorough investigation, we have no evidence to sustain the charges lately made against the Dean, Faculty and Professors of the College, but find that these charges, while in the first instance warranting investigation, are without proof; and

WHEREAS, we feel that these gentlemen have been wronged in name and reputation by the interpretation which we put upon their actions, and that an equally public acknowledgement of the same is the only proper method of repairing this wrong; therefore,

Resolved, That we do apologize to the Dean, to Professor Sloane, and to the Faculty for our former action.

On March 4th, 1884, the anonymous letter appeared. Every man received one in his mail. Discussion was at once rife. It seemed as if the letter had set a match to the smouldering embers of the discontent so rife throughout the College. In a mass-meeting at Mercer Hall, men, influenced and biased by their feelings, gave testimony which was really only hearsay evidence. A committee was appointed to draw up the first of the two sets of resolutions. In the evening another meeting was held. The resolutions were adopted by acclamation, and the committee then set out to obtain legal proof. This was not forthcoming. Dr. Murray and Prof. Sloane cleared themselves completely of the charges which were made. Investigation showed that facts and rumors had been mistaken and distorted. Nothing remained to be done but to pass the second set of resolutions and apologize. The thunder-storm, though serious for a time, certainly cleared the air. There had been some grounds for the uneasy feeling of discontent which had pervaded the College. There had also been some grounds for the great severity and strictness which the Faculty had shown during the past year. Both parties came out of the affair with a better, kinder feeling for the other. The pleasant and close relations which existed between our Class and the Faculty in Senior year I consider as partly due to the unfortunate incident which had its good results in this way. For out of evil good sometimes comes.

Classmates, Senior year has come and gone; third term has passed like a dream. No more shall we sit and sing our songs and watch the play of light and shade under the lofty elms. The plans and passions and interests of this little college world are fading into indistinctness. These four college years of which, as school boys, we saw visions and dreamt dreams which men worn and wearied with their life-battle look back upon with a regretful longing and romantic tenderness, are over, and they never can come again. We cannot travel them over again whether the path we walked by here were straight or crooked; the wicket-gate will soon be closed behind us and we cannot go back. We are to start again now. But still the joyful scenes and times, the pleasant days that are no more, will come up in long review. In this History I have tried to bring out more clearly than has been done in former years the individuality of each of our members. Yet as a class we have fought our battle here together. No division has broken our unity. Hand in hand, shoulder to shoulder, we have stood. Though we have lost many we have gained many, who have become merged in our whole. But now we are to separate. Each one is to struggle alone with his burden on his back onward, I hope upward, along his life-journey. And before we separate, at the parting of the paths, I bid to each one of you, classmates, a long farewell.

www.ingramcontent.com/pod-product-compliance
Lightning Source LLC
Chambersburg PA
CBHW020154170426
43199CB00010B/1028